DIGITAL ELECTRONIC MUSIC SYNTHESIZERS

Second Edition

No. 2695
$21.95

DIGITAL ELECTRONIC MUSIC SYNTHESIZERS

Second Edition

Delton T. Horn

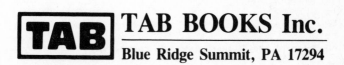 **TAB BOOKS Inc.**
Blue Ridge Summit, PA 17294

SECOND EDITION

FIRST PRINTING

Copyright © 1988 by TAB BOOKS Inc.

First edition © 1980 by TAB BOOKS Inc.

Printed in the United States of America

Library of Congress Cataloging in Publication Data

Horn, Delton T.
    Digital electronic music synthesizers.

    Rev. ed. of: Electronic music synthesizers.
1st ed. c1980.
    Includes index.
    1. Synthesizer (Musical instrument) I. Horn,
Delton, T. Electronic music synthesizers. II. Title.
ML1092.H67 1987   789.9'9   87-18108
ISBN 0-8306-9695-4
ISBN 0-8306-2695-6 (pbk.)

Questions regarding the content of this book
should be addressed to:

    Reader Inquiry Branch
    Editorial Department
    TAB BOOKS Inc.
    Blue Ridge Summit, PA 17294

Front Cover: Yamaha DX7IIFD, courtesy of YAMAHA MUSIC CORPORATION, U.S.A.

Contents

Preface to the Second Edition

Since the first edition of this book was published in 1980, there have been major changes in the music-synthesizer market. Of all the instruments described in the first edition, only some of the PAIA kits are still being manufactured. Important companies like Arp and EML have gone out of business. I haven't even heard anything from Moog in the last few years. As far as I can tell, they also have ceased production.

Even more significantly, the synthesizers of today are fundamentally different from those of a few years ago. In 1980, all synthesizers were analog designs. Today, the majority use at least some digital circuitry. Many have no dedicated modules (single-function circuitry) at all.

The introduction of the MIDI interface in 1983 created a further revolution. Now most instruments from most manufacturers can be combined to form a customized super-instrument.

With all these changes in the field, it was clearly time for a new edition of this book. Once again, no attempt was made to cover the field completely. That would be impractical and almost instantly outdated. Instead, the section on commercial synthesizers presents an overview of what is available today.

Introduction

There should be little question that synthesizers hold a major place in today's world of music. In the classroom and in popular music and commercial jingles, as well as in serious music, the synthesizer is playing an ever increasing role.

This book is intended to familiarize the reader with just what a synthesizer is and what it can do. I've included a number of construction projects, and I encourage the hobbyist to experiment with these circuits and discover his own unique variations.

I've also included an overview of some of the synthesizers that are commercially available. This is by no means a comprehensive catalog, but I feel the instruments I deal with in the text are representative of the field. This section is intended to help the reader choose between commercially available synthesizers, and to give him a better idea of just what these various synthesizers can do.

Throughout the book—and especially in Appendix A—I've included sample patch diagrams that can be duplicated on most synthesizers. Again experimentation and variations are encouraged.

Electronic music is just barely emerging from its infancy. It is frequently stunningly different from all music of the past, so many label it "unnatural."

But think of what the impact must have been when keyboards first appeared (for just one example). What an odd, indirect, *mechanical* way to attempt to produce music, for with a keyboard the musician doesn't directly produce the sound himself by blowing or striking. Instead, a machine comes between the musician and the music, with the machine striking the strings. How unnatural!

Actually, unnatural is pretty much a meaningless term in this context. After all, what's natural about plucking taut strings or blowing air through columns of metal or wood?

The important question is this—is it musical? Does it sound good and is it capable of producing an artistic response?

Properly played, a synthesizer is capable of some very beautiful, very moving and very musical sounds. Poorly played (as it is all too often), it can make some quite disturbing, earsplitting, and totally unmusical noises. But precisely the same thing can be said about the violin!

Musicality resides in the performer and the composer; it does not reside in the instrument. Musical instruments are merely tools used to produce sounds. It is up to the artist to do something musical with these instruments.

Theoretically, a synthesizer can produce an infinite number of different sounds, and can duplicate any sound—either heard or imagined. I say "theoretically," because in practice this would require an infinite (or nearly infinite) number of oscillators, filters, amplifiers and other electronic circuit stages.

There are some sounds that are possible to produce on a synthesizer, but they are so difficult and time-consuming to set up it would probably be a better idea to just bring in the original instrument you're trying to imitate and use it instead of the synthesizer. In some cases, the most profitable solution is a dedicated circuit designed just to produce a specific sound or group of related sounds. Still, the number of sounds a typical synthesizer is actually capable of producing far exceeds any number I'd want to count.

A lot of people are somewhat put off the first time they are faced with a synthesizer. All those knobs, switches and patch cords tend to frighten them, and they quickly declare that they'll never be able to operate the darn thing; it's much too complicated.

Actually, it's really rather easy to coax some kind of initial sound out of a well-designed, modern synthesizer. Just take things one step at a time and you'll be OK. Remember that the VCO (voltage controlled oscillator) usually produces a sound or signal, and most of the other sections modify that signal in some way. It's as basic as that. See Chapter 2.

The infinite claims mentioned earlier tend to frighten people, too. It's just as easy to say that there's an infinite number of rhythm patterns you can beat out on a simple homemade drum. Many sounds can quickly be discarded as not worth hearing, and even a larger number can be thought of as variations on a few basic types.

The same thing applies to the sounds produced by synthesizers. If you just sit down and play with it for awhile, you'll be surprised at how quickly you can find a few sounds that you like and can use. And once you find a few, they soon point the way to variations of themselves. In time, you'll have quite a healthy collection of usable sounds from which to choose.

I want to point out two things to all beginning synthesists. First, whenever you come up with a sound you like, jot down the way you patched it (a *patch* is the way the synthesizer is hooked up and the positions of its controls in producing a specific sound). You might want to reuse the sound or perhaps some variation of it later and you might not be able to remember how you originally achieved the effect. For this reason, you'll probably want to keep a loose-leaf notebook or set of note cards handy whenever you work with your synthesizer. Second, don't try to use everything on your synthesizer in every voice you try to create. Trying to keep track of everything and drawing up patch diagrams will quickly drive you nuts. Besides, it's actually the simpler sounds that usually sound the best and are the most useful. All those other goodies are there to provide versatility in variations of the basic sounds and to create separate sounds.

If you're trying to duplicate specific "real world" sounds, things get a bit more complex. The overtone patterns of most acoustic instruments are complex and must be in the proper phase relationship for an exact reproduction. If imitating existing instruments is your primary aim, you'd probably be better off looking at units featuring factory-wired preset voices. On the other hand, if *exact* imitation is not required, a pretty good approximation can usually be patched in.

Remember, that it's fairly easy to create sounds on a synthesizer, but to get a *specific*, predetermined sound might or might not be easy, depending on the synthesizer used, and the complexity of the desired sound (not to mention the level of your patience as sometimes it takes a bit of tinkering to get the exact effect you want).

Even if you're mainly interested in the construction projects in Part 2, I suggest you read Chapters 1 and 2. As a matter of fact, it would be a good idea to read all of Part 1. It could give you some ideas in using the circuits found in Part 2 and even in deciding which ones to build.

Part 1
The Basics of Sound Synthesis

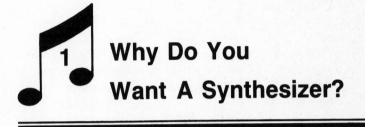

Why Do You Want A Synthesizer?

The main purpose of this book is to help you select the synthesizer that's right for you, and then help you get started with it once you've got it. I'm not going to say, "This unit is better than that unit," because frankly, virtually all synthesizers on the market today are pretty good. It's just that they're good for different purposes and tastes. Oh, I'm sure there are a few junk models out there someplace, or soon will be—some companies are just out for a fast buck—but I haven't come across any myself. In a field like this a lemon isn't likely to have much staying power on the market.

What I hope to accomplish in this part is to show you how to look at what a manufacturer says about his product, and use that information to determine whether that particular machine is right for you. I'll try to keep things open-ended enough to make my comments applicable to all other units not specifically mentioned here.

This is not an attempt to definitively catalogue what's on the market, or even the best of what's available. Such an attempt would be subject to obsolescence before the ink had a chance to dry. Instead, I've chosen several models that I feel are typical and that will probably be around for a while (or at least some similar model will be available).

The point to all this is that with what synthesizers cost, you ought to make very sure you're not getting the wrong machine.

Many commercially available units could probably be quickly eliminated from your consideration if you know what you're looking for. That way you can spend more time making a careful, thought-out choice between models that will do the job you want your synthesizer to do.

So the first question you have to ask yourself is why you want a synthesizer in the first place and what will it be used for? Here are some possibilities:

- To teach or learn about music and orchestration.
- To produce sound effects for plays, films, radio programs, etc.
- To take the place of an orchestra when the budget won't allow for more than one or two musicians—for example, in making advertising jingles for small companies or local broadcasting stations.
- To make in-studio tapes of compositions.
- For live stage performances, and possibly touring.
- For hobby purposes and fun.
- As an aid for composing so you can hear your compositions without going out and hiring an orchestra or band.
- To learn about the electronic circuitry used to produce sounds and unusual waveforms.
- To frighten dogs and small children with grotesque noises!

There are probably dozens of other reasons someone might want a synthesizer. Except for the last one, all the reasons just listed can be perfectly valid reasons for owning a synthesizer, but probably not the same synthesizer. To expect a single machine to have all these features would be a bit farfetched, no matter what the state of technology. A synthesizer used for live stage performances should be relatively lightweight, rugged and easy to patch quickly, even if this means leaving out a few devices. This would not be true of a synthesizer intended for studio use.

So stop now and think for a minute why you want a synthesizer. You may have more than one reason, so compromises might have to be made. Now is the time to decide what features and functions are important to you, for once you get to the dealer's showroom these decisions become a lot harder. And that's the function of Part One.

If your primary goal is in learning about synthesizer circuitry you'll probably want to go with kits, or projects such as those described in Part Two.

Once you've decided what you want, remember it! It's very easy to get sidetracked by some fancy feature that looks nifty but won't do you much good in achieving your primary goals.

2 Components of an Analog Synthesizer

What follows is a little refresher section on the main components of an analog synthesizer system. I won't be going into any great depth, but I will be giving some information you'll need to be familiar with to follow my later discussions.

Even if you feel you're fairly well versed in the subject, please at least skim through this chapter as I'll be making some specific suggestions of what to look for in individual sections of a synthesizer. I'll also be offering some advice on how to use some of the components.

JUST WHAT IS A SYNTHESIZER?

Before we go on, I think I should pause to define just what is meant by the term synthesizer. In the early days of electronic music, everything was done in studios filled with free standing modules and miscellaneous equipment which was interconnected via patchcords.

All a synthesizer is—in the broadest sense—is a self-contained electronic music studio. All of the various oscillators, filters, amplifiers and what not are contained within a single package.

Another difference is that a modern synthesizer generally has provisions for a keyboard or some other means of dynamically controlling the pitch (or virtually any other parameter of the sound) in real-time, whereas the classic studio techniques of the past usually

6

involved stopping the tape between each note or aural event and readjusting several controls. Most synthesizers operate through some system of voltage control where a control voltage effectively adjusts the various controls on the modules for you.

Real-time performance isn't the only advantage of voltage control. Classic studio techniques required the electronic musician to control each and every parameter of the sound he was working on manually. Voltage control can not only allow more parameters to be changed simultaneously, but it can also make the adjustments much faster and much more precisely than manual control could ever be capable of; thereby opening up all sorts of new sounds and aural events.

In other words, synthesizers provide a vastly more convenient and efficient means of reaching the musical ends. Particularly since, as I said earlier, most modern synthesizers are capable of operating (at least to some extent) in real-time, you can actually hear the passage you're working on as you're executing it. And that is a big advantage.

PATCH CORDS OR NORMALIZATION?

Most of the first commercially available synthesizers continued to use patch cords, and many still do. Today, however, most units utilize some form of normalization.

In a normalized synthesizer the manufacturer determines what are the most useful interconnections (in his opinion) and permanently hard wires them. Selection of sounds and effects is then made through the settings of various switches and knobs (pots). A typical normalization scheme is that of PAIA's Gnome microsynthesizer, shown in Fig. 2-1. (See also Chapter 6.)

Normalization undeniably limits you, but most of the more commonly used sounds can be readily produced through just such a standard patching arrangement anyway, so it's not really too big a disadvantage for many musicians. The major advantage is that specific sounds can usually be located and varied quickly and easily without having to fight your way through several miles of tangled patch cords. On the other hand, external patch cords are much more versatile, particularly if you're going after unusual or very complex sounds. They are more readily compatible with add-ons, system expansion and interfacing with other instruments or equipment. (See also the section on interfacing later in this chapter.)

If you're not sure which system to use, or feel you could use

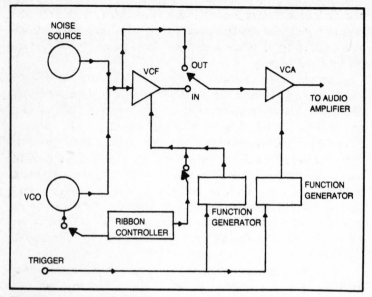

Fig. 2-1. A typical normalization scheme used in PAIA's Gnome Micro-synthesizer.

the advantages of both, some units are available that do offer both patch cords and normalization simultaneously. Ordinarily, system interconnections are hard wired through some normalization scheme, but when special effects are called for, the normalized connections can be overridden, usually with external patch cords. Arp, for example, favored this sort of arrangement.

Generally speaking, normalization is best adapted to live stage work and anywhere else where portability and patching speed is a primary concern. Patch cords are usually preferred in studio work where they're not such a nuisance, and provide a lot more versatility. For a teaching unit, either system can be adequate, provided it is clear just what paths the signal is taking—where it's going, and where it's coming from.

CONTROLLERS: KEYBOARD, RIBBON OR WHAT?

One of the first features to consider when looking at synthesizers is how is it controlled. Although not necessarily the best method of control, the most common is with some sort of a keyboard.

There are numerous advantages to using a keyboard to control a synthesizer: they're easy to relate to musically for those who are coming from a more or less traditional musical background; they're easy to write for on standard music manuscript paper; and the traditional grouping of white and black keys makes them easy to comprehend visually.

There are some disadvantages, though: keyboards are usually locked into a 12-tone system, making microtonal tunings difficult (though not always impossible); and since they are so firmly based on traditional music there is a strong tendency on the part of composer or performers to use them in a traditional manner. For example, there's really no reason why they have to be used to control just the pitch of oscillators. You could also use the keyboard (or just about any other synthesizer controller, of course) to vary the amplitude of the voltage-controlled amplifier, or the resonance of a filter, or almost any other parameter that can be put under voltage control. This literally includes almost everything in a modern synthesizer.

Another common controller for synthesizers is a *ribbon controller*. This is a strip of a special resistive material that produces a different voltage at each point along its length. With a ribbon controller it's extremely easy to glide smoothly from tone to tone, and to play between traditional pitches. However, it's usually difficult to determine precisely what pitch (or whatever) you'll get out of any specific point on the ribbon because there are no markings or visual indications to guide you. This problem is multiplied by the fact that the electrical length of a ribbon controller (the distance between the lowest and the highest available voltages) is usually variable—typically from about one to a little over four octaves.

The more versatile units often have both a keyboard and a ribbon controller. The keyboard is usually used in more or less the normal manner, while the ribbon is used to provide glides, vibrato, and between note pitches.

Another form of control that appears occasionally is the joystick, which is a three-dimensional pot, or variable control, that adjusts the relative magnitude of two or four signals or control voltages. A joystick can be quite useful in producing certain special effects, but long term use could be dangerous to your sanity. Joysticks are next to impossible to find specific settings with any kind of reasonable accuracy. Probably the most valid use of a joystick is to create three-dimensional spatial effects in a stereo or quadriphonic recording. So far as I know, no commercially available synthesizer is controlled solely by a joystick.

Another popular form of secondary control is a *sequencer*. As the name implies, a sequencer produces a sequence of control voltages. Sequencers are most often used to provide regular, reappearing rhythmic and melodic patterns.

One of the most important things to consider is the number of available sequential positions. The more positions available, the longer the pattern can be before repeating itself. Sixteen is a typical number of positions for a sequencer. Make sure some of the positions can be individually cut out of the pattern when you need different length sequences. Sixteen notes, for example, is great for ⅔ or ¼ time, but almost completely useless in ¾. Switching one of the sequential positions out of the circuit would leave 15 tones, of 5 measures of ¾ time.

Some of the more deluxe sequencers available today have provisions for setting different time lengths for each individual sequential position. That feature can provide for a lot more versatility and less monotony in the pattern.

Most sequencers have an overall speed control that adjusts how fast the sequence will be played. The wider the range is, the better. Many are capable of such high speeds that the ear can't distinguish the separate events, and some amazingly complex tones with unique sideband arrangements can be produced. Most voltage-controlled oscillators will accept a control voltage signal from both the sequencer and the keyboard (and possibly even a third source—say, for vibrato) simultaneously. Therefore, you can play a tune with your complex tone, and the sidebands will maintain the same relationship with each other, no matter what the fundamental pitch is. Of course, the same sort of techniques could also be applied to a voltage-controlled filter or a voltage-controlled amplifier.

MONOPHONIC, DUOPHONIC OR POLYPHONIC?

Most current synthesizers are monophonic; that is, they play only one note at a time, making them a solo instrument like a flute or a horn. For most purposes this is fine, because many electronically produced voices blur the distinction between complex tones and chords anyway.

But sometimes, chords as such are desirable. In a monophonic unit with multiple oscillators, three or more of the oscillators can usually be set at intervals to produce a chord each time a key is depressed. Unfortunately, once set, the intervals are fixed and constant. For example, if pressing a C on the keyboard produces a C major chord in root form, pressing F would produce an F major chord in root form, B♭ would play a B♭ major chord in root form, and so forth. Musically, that can get incredibly monotonous.

The answer to this problem, of course, is a polyphonic synthesizer. Unfortunately, there are a few technical reasons that make a polyphonic unit rather difficult to design at best. To realize the full potentialities of a synthesizer in a polyphonic unit would virtually require a complete monophonic synthesizer wired to each and every key of the keyboard. Besides being prohibitively expensive and bulky, each voice would theoretically have to be set individually for each key—not a very inviting proposition.

Fortunately, progress has been made in recent years—notably in the Polymoog (see Chapter 4). An integrated circuit mini-synthesizer is wired to each key, and master controls determine the voicing for all chips simultaneously. This ingenious design took several years to bring into reality.

A few other polyphonic synthesizers are on the market, but remember that polyphonic capabilities increase the relative cost drastically, and usually tend to reduce the amount of available versatility in voicing. So stop and think about just how important chords are to you before jumping on the polyphonic bandwagon.

As a sort of a halfway measure you might want to take a look at what are known as duophonic, or multiphonic synthesizers. In the simplest duophonic units two complete monophonic synthesizers can be set to the same, or contrasting voices. Of course in multiphonic synthesizers there are more monophonic subunits.

Usually the keyboard is scanned digitally. When a key is found to be depressed, the voltage and trigger information from that key is sent to one of the monophonic subunits for processing. Then the digital scanning continues. For further information on this approach, see the chapter on the Oberheim units.

I've been speaking of keyboards here, primarily because something like a ribbon controller, by its very nature, tends to be monophonic. It's probably the very presence of keyboards on so many synthesizers that has been the biggest factor in the push for polyphonic units in the first place. Traditional keyboard instruments are polyphonic, so there is an assumption that a keyboard synthesizer should also be polyphonic. You have to decide for yourself whether or not that assumption is true for you.

THE VCO

The VCO, or voltage-controlled oscillator is one of the most

11

fundamental components in a synthesizer. Most voicings will start with a VCO.

The most common setup is for the VCO to accept a voltage signal from the keyboard or other controller and use it to produce a pitched output that is then processed by the other components. You can produce music of some sort with just a controller and a VCO, but the limitations of such a simple patch should be rather obvious.

One of the first things to look for in a VCO is how many outputs it has, and what kind they are. Some common waveforms are shown in Fig. 2-2. Probably the most useful—and most common—are the

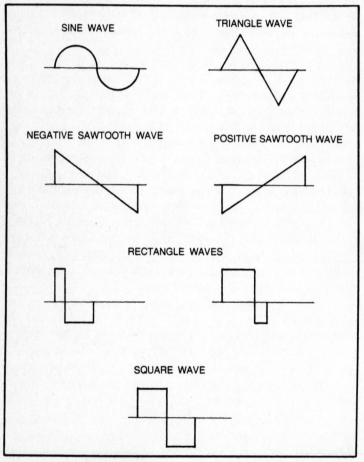

Fig. 2-2. Some typical waveshapes.

triangle and the square wave, which is a special form of the rectangular or pulse wave. By themselves, the triangle wave sounds rather like a flute, and the square wave has a nice, reedy sound. However, what really makes these wave shapes so useful is that they both have a rather high amount of harmonic content.

If you're at all familiar with acoustics—and you should have some footing in the subject if you want to get much more than unidentifiable noises out of most synthesizers—you know that a pure tone without any harmonics is extremely rare, or actually nonexistent, in the real world. Harmonics play a tremendous part in determining why a guitar doesn't sound much like a clarinet. (There are several other factors too, of course, but we can consider them irrelevant at this point.) In most modern synthesis techniques, it's desirable to start out with a waveform that's rich in harmonics and then filter out the ones you don't want.

A sine wave produces a pure tone. After listening to a solo sine wave for a few minutes, you'll probably be grateful it doesn't pop up too much in nature; a pure tone is rather hard to take all by itself. Sine waves are mainly used as control signals in such effects as *tremolo* or *vibrato*, and in these applications a sine wave usually sounds better than any other waveshape.

If a multitude of sine wave oscillators are available, you can use what is known as *additive synthesis*. Instead of filtering out the harmonics you don't want, you add in the ones you *do* want. On the surface, that sounds like a more logical method, but for any kind of tone complexity at all so many oscillators would be necessary that it would hardly be worth the expense and effort. Generally, *subtractive* (filtering) *synthesis* is greatly preferred.

One advantage of additive techniques is that you can create nonharmonic overtones along with the harmonic ones. Many sounds, such as certain bells and chimes, require nonharmonic overtones to make them sound natural.

If you don't quite understand what the terms *harmonic* and *non-harmonic* mean, take a look at Fig. 2-3. Starting with A below middle C, the figure shows a harmonic overtone series, and a non-harmonic pattern. In a harmonic overtone series, all the component tones are multiples of the fundamental root frequency. When you have a certain frequency F, the second harmonic is 2 times F, the third harmonic is 3 times F, the fourth is 4 times F, and so on. A nonharmonic series can be anything that doesn't fit within that pattern.

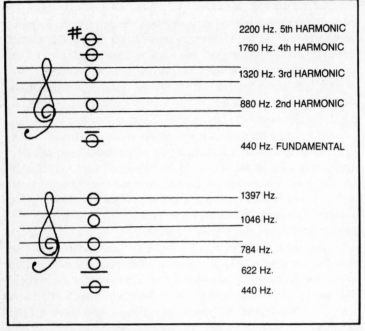

Fig. 2-3. Harmonic and nonharmonic overtones.

There's certainly no reason why you can't combine both additive and subtractive synthesis at the same time. If you start with, say, three square waves at frequencies that don't bear any specific harmonic relationship with each other, you'll then have plenty of nonharmonic overtones to choose from, filtering out the ones you don't want.

Perhaps even more useful than the triangle or square wave is the *ramp*, or *sawtooth*, wave. Unfortunately, this type wave is not as common. The triangle and square waves have only the odd harmonics (F, 3F, 5F, 7F . . .), whereas the ramp has both odd and even harmonics (F, 2F, 3F, 4F . . .).

Another nice feature would be a switch of some kind to select between either a positive or negative sawtooth wave (see Fig. 2-2). Besides producing two distinct and different sounds, the two forms could be extremely useful as control signals.

Many synthesizers feature a *variable width*, or *variable duty cycle*, rectangular wave which can be varied from a very narrow pulse to a square wave, or even further. Again, this gives you a wide range of possible outputs to choose from. And the more outputs your VCO has, the more versatile it will be.

If you have to give up at least one of the basic waveforms, the sine wave is probably the most expendable. A triangle wave can simulate most of the effects of the sine wave in low-frequency control applications, and if a real sine wave is ever really needed, you can always filter all the harmonics out of a more complex wave, leaving just the fundamental, which by itself is a sine wave, of course. As it turns out, a really good voltage-controlled sine wave oscillator is rather difficult and expensive to produce, so that's an output that is frequently left out anyway.

A voltage-controlled oscillator, by definition, has some sort of dc control voltage input, but it will usually accept an ac control signal too. If your synthesizer has this kind of capability, you can use one oscillator to frequency modulate another. When the modulating oscillator is set to a very low frequency, the result will be a vibrato or trill of some sort. The output of the second oscillator would switch instantaneously from one pitch to another—then back again—whenever a square wave is used as the modulating input. An ascending sawtooth wave would produce an output that would start at a certain frequency. This frequency increases in pitch up to some definite peak and then instantaneously reverts back to the original pitch to start all over again. A negative ramp would have precisely the opposite effect. Sine waves or triangle waves are usually used for traditional vibrato effects.

As the modulating oscillator increases in frequency, the ear can't distinguish between the separate pitches in time, and they are blended to produce a complex and probably nonharmonic overtone pattern. In addition, *sidebands* are produced above and below the fundamental frequency which exist in none of the original tones. These sidebands very rarely exhibit any harmonic relationship to the fundamental frequency, so this method is also useful for producing nonharmonic sounds. Sidebands can also be produced through amplitude modulation as well as frequency modulation, but that's a subject best discussed under the heading of "Voltage Controlled Amplifiers."

A more mundane, but absolutely essential point to look for in a VCO is the stability of its output frequency. If you can't keep the fool thing in tune over extended periods of time, it's going to be hard to use it musically. Fortunately, most modern VCOs are at least acceptably stable.

NOISE SOURCES

It would seem that noise would be something you'd want to

avoid like the plague, but a controllable noise source in a synthesizer can be used for a lot of nice special effects that would be difficult, or even impossible, to produce otherwise. The most obvious use of a noise source would be to generate such basically nonmusical sounds as wind, surf, drums, crashes, explosions, etc. But that isn't the limit to its uses. If you're trying to accurately duplicate a traditional instrument, you might find a certain amount of noise quite useful. In a wind instrument, for example, the player's breath can usually be heard buried beneath the musical tones. In a violin, the bow striking and scraping across the strings also adds a small, but definite, amount of noise to the final sound.

Noise sources are usually rather simple and inexpensive to build, so they're special effects devices that are included in most synthesizer packages.

There are two basic types of noise sources: *White noise* and *Pink noise*. White noise usually sounds rather like the interstation hiss you get if you tune an FM tuner between channels with the muting off. Pink noise is more heavily weighted towards the lower frequencies, and by itself tends to be the more pleasing sound.

Some synthesizers offer both pink and white noise sources, while others just have one or the other. If just one is available, it's better that it be a white noise source since a close approximation of pink noise can be achieved by filtering white noise, but the opposite is not possible. Nevertheless, I'd hardly make the type of noise source a deciding factor in choosing a synthesizer.

FILTERS

The filter is probably the real heart of the modern synthesizer. This is the device that makes subtractive synthesis possible.

There are four basic types of filters. A *low-pass filter* passes all tones below a certain point (the cutoff frequency) and rejects or, at least, strongly cuts back all the higher tones. A *high-pass filter* is the exact opposite. The *band-pass filter* passes a certain select band of frequencies, while stopping any tones that fall outside (above or below) that band. Its opposite is the relatively rare *band-reject filter*. As its name implies, the band-reject, or notch, filter rejects or stops a specific band of frequencies, while passing all tones above or below its selected band. The effects of the four types of filters are shown in Fig. 2-4.

The most common filter found on synthesizers is the low-pass filter. This is largely because this particular filter arrangement

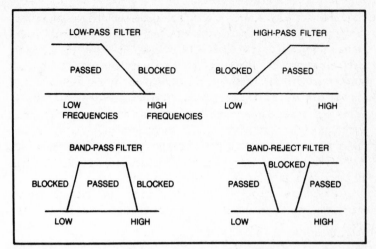

Fig. 2-4. The four types of filters used in music synthesizers.

affects only the overtones while leaving the primary fundamental frequency intact.

The band-pass filter is also extremely useful in synthesizers—particularly if its bandwidth is variable, it's probably the most versatile type. If the passed band is adjusted so that its lower cutoff point is below the limits of audibility, you'd have, in effect, a low-pass filter. Likewise, if the upper cutoff point is set above the range of audibility, a high-pass filter would be simulated. And not only would you have a choice between low and high-pass filters; the bandpass could be set anywhere between the two limits for an incredible number of different effects.

Other synthesizers have a low-pass and a high-pass filter, but no band-pass. In most cases, a little imagination will allow you to combine the two to act as though they were a single band-pass unit.

One thing to look for in filters is whether or not they're voltage-controllable. In a fixed filter the cutoff frequency is constant, so the entire overtone structure of the signal will change as the fundamental frequency changes. A voltage-controlled filter VCF, on the other hand, can track along with the oscillator in a constant relationship, keeping the overtone structure constant no matter what the fundamental frequency is. Also, most VCFs have access to control by some sort of function generator explained later to provide for special effects and timbres that change with time. This kind of temporal fluctuation of timbre is common with many traditional instruments.

One very important thing to look for in a filter is the rate, or slope, of cutoff. An ideal filter would have an infinite cutoff, so that if a low-pass filter was set at 1000 Hz, a tone at 999 Hz would be heard unaffected, while one at 1001 Hz would be completely removed from the output. Rate of cutoff is usually measured in *dB* per octave, and the higher the dB figure is, the better the filter is, generally speaking.

VOLTAGE-CONTROLLED AMPLIFIERS

Basically, a voltage-controlled amplifier (VCA) isn't much different from any other amplifier, except that instead of having a manually operated volume control, control voltages determine the amplitude of the output. You could theoretically achieve the same sort of effects with an ordinary amplifier if you could adjust the volume control fast enough and precisely enough. But because voltage control can do the job so much more efficiently, why not leave your hands free for functions that they're better at?

The two most common sources of control voltage for a VCA are an oscillator of some sort and a function, or envelope, generator. Generally, the oscillator will produce a periodic amplitude envelope. The waveshape of the control oscillator can actually be heard at very low control frequencies. For example, a positive sawtooth wave would cause a smooth, steady increase in volume up to a specific peak and then drop right back down to the original minimum point and start over. A rectangular wave would switch instantaneously back and forth between the minimum and maximum levels with no intermediate points. As the frequency of the control oscillator is increased into the audible region, the ear is no longer able to detect the fluctuations in volume, and—just as in frequency modulation—sidebands are created. This is called *amplitude modulation*. While similar in principle to frequency modulation, amplitude modulation has different, distinctive sound qualities.

A function generator is usually triggered by the keyboard, sequencer or whatever to produce a single envelope around each individual note. For example, if you were trying to simulate the sound of a guitar, the function generator would be set to provide a very sharp attack (increase in volume from 0 to maximum), very little sustain (the time the maximum level is held), and a moderately slow decay (decrease in volume back down to zero). A wind instrument, on the other hand, would have a slower attack and might be capable of considerable sustain times. Usually the changes in volume are quicker than the ear can catch them individually, but the amplitude envelope can have a very major effect on how that voice sounds.

FUNCTION OR ENVELOPE GENERATORS

A function or envelope generator accepts a trigger signal from the keyboard or other controller and produces an output voltage that varies in time. In its simplest form it has two controls: attack and decay. Figure 2-5 illustrates some typical attack/decay patterns.

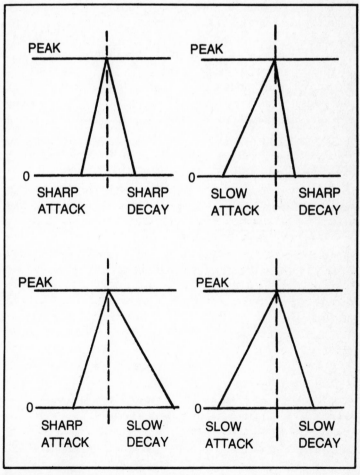

Fig. 2-5. Typical attack/decay envelopes.

As useful as attack and decay are, it is usually desirable to be able to hold the note at its maximum level for some specific length of time. This is referred to as *sustain*. Some function generators have a sustain time control, but most employ the more practical method of holding the note for as long as the key is depressed. The decay is initiated when the key is released. By far, this is the more useful system musically, because after all, in music different notes last for different amounts of time (whole notes, half notes, quarter notes, etc.). Figure 2-6 shows an attack/sustain/decay envelope. Figure 2-7 shows an attack/decay/sustain/release envelope.

Another control frequently found on function generators is a *preliminary decay* control. In this sort of arrangement, the voltage builds to a maximum level at a rate determined by the attack control and then decays to some preset level which is held, or sustained, until the key is released. The signal is then dropped back to zero at a rate determined by the final decay or release control. This type of function generator is known as an ADSR (attack/decay/sustain/release) generator. The most common use of a function generator is to provide the control voltage to a VCA or VCF, but it could also conceivably control a VCO.

INTERFACING

Many synthesizers, particularly the smaller, portable ones, are entirely self-contained with no capabilities for expansion. For some

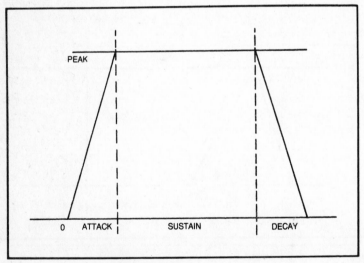

Fig. 2-6. Attack/sustain/decay envelope.

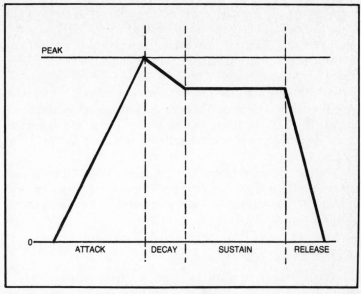

Fig. 2-7. Attack/decay/sustain/release envelope.

users this is fine, but many others might want the capability to add more synthesizer functions as they are developed, or as budget allows. If you're going to be interested in possible expansion, make sure that the unit you choose has add-on capabilities. On the other hand, if you're just interested in the basic synthesizer functions, and want to keep everything simple, don't bother about add-ons. Keep in mind, though, that certain accessories, such as foot pedals and the like, can come in very handy at times.

Another point to consider is whether the synthesizer can process other external instruments. Many units have electric guitar and/or microphone inputs to make a wide range of additional voices easily available from practically any source. In most cases, this feature probably isn't necessary, although it's nice to have. Why laboriously synthesize an electric guitar sound so you can further process it when you can just plug in a real guitar and take it from there. If you primarily play guitar, some synthesizers designed specifically to use an electric guitar input as their primary signal source are available.

PRESETS

A lot of synthesizers these days have preset voices available at the flick of a switch. Some typical voices are flute, strings, piano, harpsichord and "outer space sounds." These presets are helpful when fast changes between standard and often difficult to patch voicings are required. But watch out—presets can often throw you into a limitation trap that leaves you with nothing more versatile than a souped-up organ.

When trying out a synthesizer, listen to the preset voices, if any. Do you like the sound of most of them enough to use them frequently? Are there capabilities for synthesizing your own original sounds? Can the preset voices be altered in any usable way? If so, how much?

I'm not against preset voices per se; sometimes they can be a real help. But if you can't create your own unique, original voicings, you're missing out on a lot of what synthesizers are all about in the first place.

SOUND SYSTEMS

The sound system is just the amplifier and speaker(s) that make it possible for you to actually hear what you're synthesizing. But that's a big "just," because your synthesizer is only going to sound as good as the system you're playing it through.

So get the best sound system you can afford. Oh, if you have to scrimp a little at the time of original purchase, you can cheat a little, but get a better sound system as soon as possible. You can always use an extra practice amp, and especially speakers, but getting a cheap synthesizer only to replace it with a better model later is rather wasteful. This isn't always true as sometimes a small second synthesizer can be nice to have for those super-duper voices. However, you should still start with your main unit first and build around that. It makes a lot more sense.

You really have to be careful in choosing speakers for a synthesizer system. Since most synthesizers produce frequencies well outside either end of the audio spectrum, the fatality rate for speakers can be alarmingly high if you don't watch out. High levels of very low subaudio, or very high ultra-audio, signals can totally pulverize a cheap speaker in a matter of seconds. The safest method would be to choose wide-range speakers that can handle about 25 percent to 40 percent more power than the amplifier can put out. They should be reasonably immune then. On the other hand, you have to make sure the amp has enough power to drive them efficiently. It's a tricky business.

You'll probably blow a few speakers from time to time, despite all precautions, so it's a good idea to keep some spares. It's probably also a good idea to split the output of the amplifier into several speakers so that the total power is spread out among them. And definitely use a woofer/tweeter arrangement. Particularly with the wide frequency range of a synthesizer, the so-called full-range speakers simply don't make the grade.

RECORDING

Most synthesists are interested in recording their audio creations, perhaps building up multilayered compositions consisting of several separate voices, so a few words on recorders are in order. First off, get a reel-to-reel, or open-reel, tape recorder. Cassettes are convenient, but they're almost impossible to edit. You might want to dub the end result onto a cassette for a final copy, but that isn't the kind of recording we're concerned with here.

For multiple voice recording you need at the very least a good two- or four-track deck with some kind of synchronization abilities.

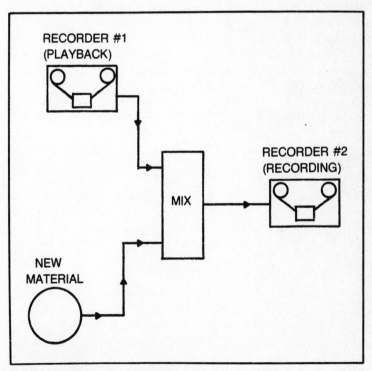

Fig. 2-8. A two-recorder mixing setup.

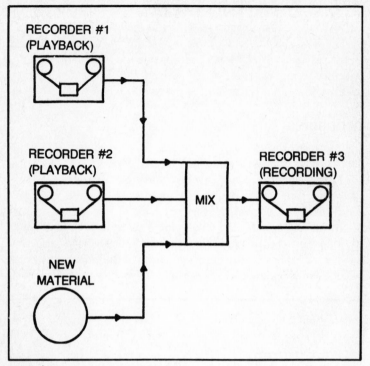

RECORDER #1
(PLAYBACK)

RECORDER #2
(PLAYBACK)

RECORDER #3
(RECORDING)

MIX

NEW
MATERIAL

Fig. 2-9. A three-recorder mixing setup.

If you can't keep all the parts in sync with each other, the whole thing is going to sound rather chaotic at best.

You don't need a big studio eight- or sixteen-track recorder. They'd make the job a lot easier, but they're prohibitively expensive for most people—even more expensive than many of the synthesizers themselves. As it turns out, you can do just about everything the big machines can do with just a decent mixer and two or more smaller recorders. Figures 2-8 and 2-9 show some possible mixing setups with two or three recorders. While the recorders in the drawing are stereo (two-channel), a four-channel deck would greatly increase the capabilities.

If your decks have self-sync switches, each of the playback recorders can have two or four separate parts on them—sometimes even more—before even getting to the mixer stage. This is more than a slight advantage, particularly when many different parts are involved, since the more times you re-record a passage, the more noise you pick up along the way.

3 Digital Sound Synthesis

In the last chapter we studied the various modules (circuits) that make up an analog sound synthesizer. In recent years, more and more commercial synthesizers are based on digital rather than analog circuitry.

In a purely digital system, there are no actual modules as such. Instead, the functions of the various analog modules (VCOs, VCFs, VCAs, envelope generators, and so forth) are simulated by computer software. Any combination of modules can be readily programmed. Additional circuitry does not have to be hard-wired into the system. Modifications are made through changes in the software. Switching between one voice to another can be done almost instantly, no matter how differently the "module" setup. The "modules" and all their parameters (control settings) required for a given voice can be stored in computer memory for instant recall at any time.

We will now take a quick look at how a computer can digitally simulate each of the basic analog sound synthesis modules.

THE DIGITAL VCO

We will start with the digital equivalent to the VCO, since this is the starting point for the signal that will eventually be a sound. Some manufacturers refer to a digital equivalent of the VCO as a *DCO* (Digitally-Controlled Oscillator), but this term has not yet found universal acceptance.

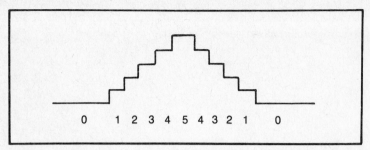

Fig. 3-1. A periodic string of numbers generated by a computer can be fed through a D/A converter to produce a digitally generated triangle wave.

A periodic (repeating pattern) string of numbers generated by a computer can be fed through a *D/A* (Digital to Analog) *converter* to produce an ac signal. A sample output from such a system is shown in Fig. 3-1.

Any waveshape created in this manner will inevitably have the characteristic sharp edged steps of a digital signal. This means that all such waveforms will have an extremely strong harmonic content. The sound will tend to be quite raspy. In some cases this may be exactly what we want. But more often, it will be too limited for sound synthesis applications.

The solution is to smooth out the sharp edges of the waveform by passing it through a simple low-pass filter. A moderately large valued capacitor across the output will generally be sufficient. Figure 3-2 shows the signal from Fig. 3-1 after it has been capacitively filtered. We now have a digitally generated triangle wave, which

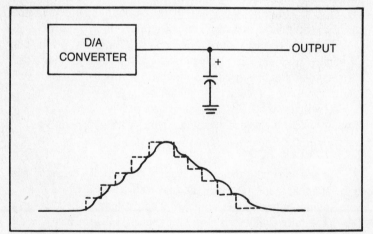

Fig. 3-2. The ac signal in Figure 3-1 can be improved with a filter capacitor.

has a very weak harmonic content. (In many non-critical applications, triangle waves can be substituted for sine waves.)

By outputting the right sequence of numbers, a computer can generate literally any waveform imaginable—all with the same circuitry. Only the programming must be changed. This is certainly far more versatile than any analog oscillator circuit.

The output waveform is sampled at a regular rate—X times per second. The higher the value of X, the greater detail there can be in the final output signal. X must be at least twice the highest frequency component to be used. If X is less than twice the frequency being sampled, a phantom lower frequency signal may appear. In a sense, the D/A converter gets "confused." This is called *aliasing*.

The sampling rate of the output signal is a constant, hardware function. It is not related to the frequency of the DCO.

The DCO waveshape is defined by a sequence of numbers. The sequenced length is usually fixed for all waveshapes and frequencies. For our discussion, we will assume a sequence length of ten steps. A practical system would probably use a much longer sequence, but this short version will be more convenient for purposes of illustration.

Let's assume we are working with the digital equivalent of an ascending sawtooth wave. The sequence pattern might look like this;

0
2
4
6
8
10
13
15
17
20
0   (The sequence now repeats itself.)
2
4
8

and so on.

If we output this sequence at a sampling rate of 2000 steps per second (a practical system would have a much higher sampling rate to prevent aliasing problems), the output frequency would be equal to;

$$2000/10$$

or 200 Hz.

The output frequency is simply the sampling rate, divided by the sequence length. That is;

$$f = SR/SL$$

Now, how can we change the output frequency? We have already stated that the sampling rate and the sequence length are constants, and they are the only factors in the output equation.

Actually the sequence length is fixed in the computer's memory, where it is stored in the form of a table. But we can change the way we step through the table. So far we have looked at table entry A, then table entry $A + 1$, then table entry $A + 1 + 1$, and so on. To change the output frequency, we simply change the step factor for looking at entries in the table.

Let's say we use a step value of 2. Now the sequence we are outputting looks like this;

ENTRY #1	0
ENTRY #3	4
ENTRY #5	8
ENTRY #7	13
ENTRY #9	17
ENTRY #1	0
ENTRY #3	4
ENTRY #5	8

and so on.

Now the sequence repeats itself after five steps. This (not the table length) is used as the sequence length (SL) for the output frequency equation. We now have an output frequency of;

$$f = SR/SL = 2000/5 = 400 \text{ Hz}.$$

Now, let's try it with a step value of three. The output sequence looks like this;

ENTRY #1	0
ENTRY #4	6

```
ENTRY #7   13
ENTRY #10  20
ENTRY #3    4
ENTRY #6   10
ENTRY #9   17
ENTRY #2    2
ENTRY #5    8
ENTRY #8   15
ENTRY #1    0
ENTRY #4    6
ENTRY #7   13
```

and so on.

Notice that the sequence isn't exactly the same for each cycle through the table. This is because the table sequence length is not an integer multiple of the step value. That's perfectly all right. It might look a little confusing to us, but it presents no problem to the computer. In this case the sequence length is approximately 3.3333, so the output frequency works out to about;

$$f = 2000/3.3333 = 600.6 \text{ Hz.}$$

We can also use non-integer step values, such as 1.6. In this case we will often end up landing between actual entries in the table. There are two ways the computer can deal with this situation. It can either round off to the nearest table entry, or it can interpolate between table values. For example, if the step sequence landed us on 2.5, we'd look at the values in entry #2 and entry #3 and average them together. In our sample table, entry #2 is 2, and entry #3 is 4, so the interpolated mid-point between them is 3.

We will use the round-off method for convenience. Using a step value of 1.6 we get the following output sequence;

(1)	ENTRY #1	0
(2.6)	ENTRY #3	4
(4.2)	ENTRY #4	6
(5.8)	ENTRY #6	10
(7.4)	ENTRY #7	13
(9)	ENTRY #9	17
(0.6)	ENTRY #1	0
(3.2)	ENTRY #3	4
(4.8)	ENTRY #5	8

(6.4)	ENTRY #6	10
(8)	ENTRY #8	15
(9.6)	ENTRY #10	20
(1.2)	ENTRY #1	0

and so on.

The output sequence length is equal to the table length (TL) divided by the step rate (s);

$$SL = TL/s$$

In this case:

$$SL = 10/1.6 = 6.25$$

This gives us an output frequency of;

$$f = 2000/6.25 = 320 \text{ Hz.}$$

Suppose we need a lower output frequency than the base value (SL = s—200 Hz. in our example)? Easy. Just use a step value less than 1. For instance, if we use a step value of 0.4, we get this output sequence;

(1.0)	ENTRY #1	0
(1.4)	ENTRY #1	0
(1.8)	ENTRY #2	2
(2.2)	ENTRY #2	2
(2.6)	ENTRY #3	4
(3.0)	ENTRY #3	4
(3.4)	ENTRY #3	4
(3.8)	ENTRY #4	6
(4.2)	ENTRY #4	6
(4.6)	ENTRY #5	8

and so on. To save space, we will not go through a complete cycle, which would require 25 steps. This makes the output frequency equal to;

$$f = 2000/25 = 80 \text{ Hz.}$$

Thus, any output frequency can be selected by choosing the right step value in looking up entries in the waveform table.

The waveform table itself may be constructed in any of a number of ways. Most periodic (repeating) waveforms can be expressed directly via a mathematical formula. Many interesting results can be achieved by experimenting with different equations.

Probably the most direct approach is to use a variation on the analog additive synthesis method. Remember, any waveform can be made up by combining various sine waves. A sine wave gets its name because it follows the mathematical sine function.

To use this method, you first calculate the desired angle increment (Ai), using this equation;

$$Ai = 2 \pi /TL$$

where π is the constant pi (approximately 3.14), and TL is the number of samples in the table.

For the first sample, A is set to 0. For each successive sample, A is increased by Ai. That is;

$$A = A + Ai$$

For a simple sine wave, each sample value (V) is simply the sine of A;

$$V = \sin(A)$$

For each additional frequency component, add in the sine of H (the harmonic number) × A with an appropriate scaling factor. Let's assume we want a waveform consisting of the fundamental and harmonics two through four. The relative levels of the frequency components are as follows;

FUNDAMENTAL	100%
SECOND HARMONIC	50%
THIRD HARMONIC	35%
FOURTH HARMONIC	15%

The equation for each sample value in the waveform table would be;

$$V = \sin(A) + (0.5 \times \sin(2A)) + (0.35 \times \sin(3A)) + (0.15 \times \sin(4A))$$

Clearly, these calculations can get a little awkward with pencil and paper, but they're no problems at all for a computer to handle.

DIGITAL FILTERING

Since the waveform table can be calculated with mathematical formulae, it naturally follows that it can be modified with similar formulae.

For digital filtering calculations, an accumulator is set up. We will call this R. It functions in a manner similar to an *analog integrator* (low-pass filter). Numbers are repeatedly added to the accumulator for each sample, so its value continuously changes.

To simulate a simple passive RC type filter, we need to incorporate the effects of capacitive leakage. A constant proportion of the accumulator's value is subtracted from each sample to simulate the leakage of a capacitor. The leakage constant will be called K.

In an analog filter circuit, the capacitive leakage is related to the capacitance value. The cut-off frequency is also dependent on the size of the capacitor. Similarly, in the digital filter, the cut-off frequency is determined by the value of K.

For each sample, we can calculate the accumulator's new value with this formula;

$$R = R - (K \times R) + V$$

where V is the value of the current sample from the waveform table.

For the first sample, R is assumed to have a previous value of 0.

A new table is created by applying this equation to each of the old table entries. The result will be the low-pass filtered equivalent of the original signal.

Other similar equations can be used to simulate other filter types. The digital system is not limited to the four basic analog filter types (low-pass, high-pass, band-pass, and band-reject). All sorts of unique frequency responses can be set up, just by trying different filtering equations.

THE DIGITAL AMPLIFIER

To simulate a VCA envelope digitally, each table entry is multiplied by a gain factor.

Let's say we have a waveform table with the following ten values;

0
4
8
10
5
0
− 5
− 10
− 8
− 4
0

If we use a constant gain factor of 2, each of the table values will be doubled;

0
8
16
20
10
0
− 10
− 20
− 16
− 8
0

The amplitude of the wave has been increased.

Attenuation (reduced levels) can be achieved by using a gain factor that is less than 1. For instance, if we apply a gain factor of 0.5 to the original table, we get the following values;

0
2
4
5
2.5
0
− 2.5
− 5
− 4
− 2
0

The signal now has only half its original amplitude.

The envelope generator can easily be simulated by another table of values, or a series of calculations that apply different gain factors at different times.

Any shape envelope can easily be programmed. The digital musician is not limited to the basic envelope types, like those illustrated in Fig. 3-3. In an analog synthesizer, it would certainly be difficult to come up with a complex envelope like the one shown

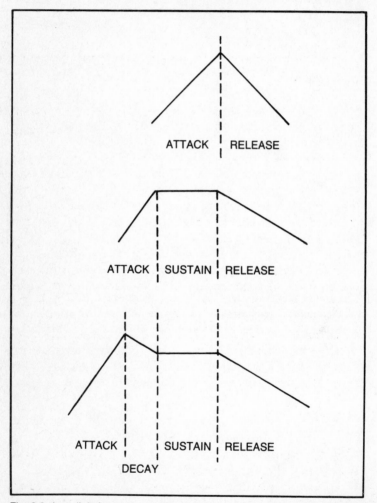

Fig. 3-3. In a digital system you are not limited to the basic analog envelope types.

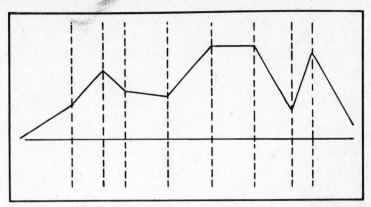

Fig. 3-4. In an analog synthesizer, it would be difficult to produce a complex envelope like this.

in Fig. 3-4. It would be no problem at all to generate such an envelope digitally. It's no more difficult than the simple traditional type envelopes.

There is one final point that should be mentioned. Notice that in the last set of examples, the waveform table included negative values. The waveform needs to be centered around zero in order for the gain factor amplification method to work properly. Fortunately, the sine calculations discussed earlier will give both positive and negative values.

Unfortunately, most D/A converters can't deal with negative numbers. Before the signal information is fed out to the D/A converter, an offset adjustment should be added to each sample value. Typically, the offset adjustment will be one half the D/A converter's full scale limit. For example, if the D/A converter can accept digital values from 0 to 255, an offset adjustment of 128 will be added to each sample. Now a value of 128 represents the zero line. The signal can range from -128 to $+127$, which should be more than adequate for most musical applications.

SUMMARY

As you can see, the computer is really very well suited for synthesis. In most cases it can do an even better job than an analog system. Digital music isn't really such a far out idea after all.

In fact, philosophers over the ages have considered music to be a branch of mathematics. Maybe digital sound synthesis isn't even a very new idea. In a sense, it is a return to our musical roots.

MIDI

In the last few years there has been a lot of excitement in the electronic music industry over MIDI—the Musical Instrument Digital Interface. This is a hardware and software standard for interfacing various synthesizers, sequencers, drum machines, tape recorders, and microcomputers. Since the basic specifications are industry standardized, equipment from different manufacturers can be combined.

The basic compatibility of MIDI hardware and software allows the musician to create an economical interactive sound synthesis system, with a great deal of power and versatility for performers, composers, and studio engineers.

MIDI HARDWARE SPECIFICATIONS

The MIDI system is designed to permit inexpensive plug in compatibility between various sound synthesis devices (synthesizers, drum machines, sequencers, mixers, microcomputers, etc.) even if they're made by different manufacturers. Previously interfacing equipment was no simple task. Some devices used positive triggering, while others used negative triggering. Some used linear control, and others used exponential control. Some had a maximum control voltage of 5 volts, while others allowed control voltages up to 10 volts.

MIDI has changed all that. If two devices are both MIDI compatible, they can be used together, at least at the most basic level. To ensure such compatibility, a number of physical factors have been exactly defined in the standards.

MIDI connections are made via a standard 5 pin DIN plug. The interface uses an opto-isolated current loop to prevent ground loops and noise pickup.

MIDI compatible equipment has two or three jacks. The basic MIDI IN circuit is illustrated in Fig. 4-1. The second jack is labelled MIDI OUT. The basic circuit is shown in Fig. 4-2.

Some devices also have a MIDI THRU jack. The basic circuit is shown in Fig. 4-3. This optional third jack produces a direct copy of incoming data (through the MIDI IN jack). The MIDI THRU jack is used for daisy chain hook-ups, like the one illustrated in Fig. 4-4. Other systems are arranged in a star network, as shown in Fig. 4-5. MIDI THRU jacks are not used in star systems.

Connecting cables should not exceed 50 feet. Shielded or twisted pair cables should be used. The shielding is connected to pin 2 at both ends. MIDI OUT jacks are grounded to the instrument

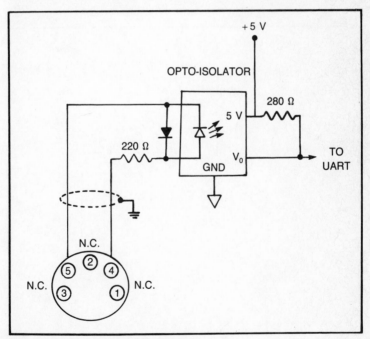

Fig. 4-1. This is the basic MIDI IN circuit.

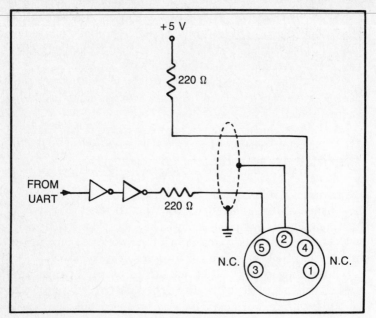

Fig. 4-2. This is the basic MIDI OUT circuit.

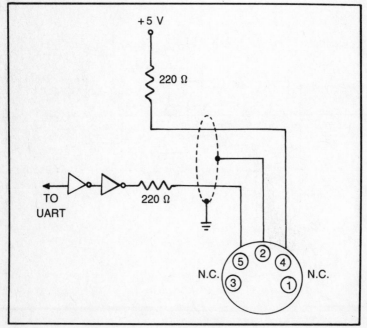

Fig. 4-3. Some devices also have a MIDI THRU circuit.

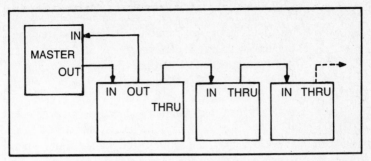

Fig. 4-4. The MIDI THRU jack is used for daisy chain hook-ups.

chasis, but MIDI IN jacks are not. This consistent approach to grounding eliminates the fear of ground loops.

Data is transmitted between devices in a specific serial format. The transmission rate is specified at 31.25 kBaud. If you don't work much with computers, this term will probably be unfamiliar to you. Don't worry about it. It's just a measurement of the speed at which data can be read from one device into another. Since it is standardized, the user can ignore it altogether. The beginning of a new

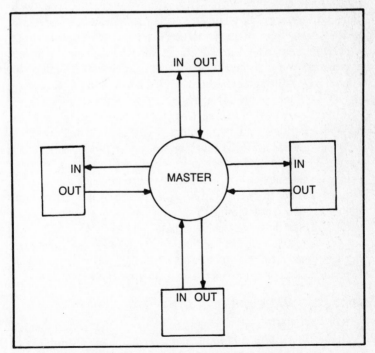

Fig. 4-5. Some MIDI systems are arranged in a star network.

note, including all parameters can take less than a millisecond (0.001 second). All the musician needs to know is that the data transmission is fast enough to appear instantaneous.

The MIDI interconnection standards are designed to minimize hum pick-up and ground loop problems that can plague a poorly thought out custom interface.

A multi-instrument system will tend to be more compact when MIDI is used. In addition, set-up will be greatly simplified. Once the system is hooked up, changes are made via software. There is no need to physically move any wires around. One hook-up fits all. Another advantage of this is the cable connections are consistent throughout the system. This lessens the chances for making a mistake.

The MIDI hardware interface requires just a few components. The cost is low enough to make adding it to any microprocessor controlled equipment more than feasible. The use of MIDI interfaces in commercial equipment should grow more and more widespread in the next few years.

The MIDI system can even lower the cost of many instruments by eliminating redundancy of expensive features, such as a touch-sensitive keyboard. A single keyboard can be used to play several synthesizers. Several manufacturers are already offering high-capability remote keyboards (without a synthesizer) and complete synthesizer expander modules (without a keyboard). The user can customize his instrument/system to fit his own individual requirements, without paying for unnecessary duplication.

In the pre-MIDI days, everything that needed a clock (synchronization signal) had a complete clock circuit built in. When multiple devices are used together, you only want a single clock signal, so all the devices are in sync with each other. The other clocks have to be disabled, and left to sit around uselessly. Rather than pay for several mediocre clock circuits, why not just buy one high-precision clock circuit to drive everything in your system? MIDI, at least in theory, allows this.

MIDI instruments and devices can be considered as modules in a customized sound synthesis system. The system can easily be expanded as your needs increase or as your budget allows.

MIDI SOFTWARE SPECIFICATIONS

The MIDI software will depend on the specific application. Essentially, MIDI is a dedicated computer language. A number of standardized commands can be combined to form various programs.

Since all MIDI equipment "speaks the same language," MIDI programs are transferable.

MIDI commands can be thought of as words grouped into phrases. For example, let's say you depress a key on the keyboard of a MIDI synthesizer. The synthesizer will play the note directly, and send a descriptive phrase about the note out through the synthesizer's MIDI port. The phrase might be something like this;

> Note Event: ON
> Pitch: A'
> Velocity: 5

A second phrase is sent out when the key is released.

If a sequencer is connected to the MIDI port of this synthesizer, it can be set to record this data. The synthesizer is the sender, and the sequencer is the receiver.

Later, the sequencer can be set for playback. Now the sequencer will function as the sender and the synthesizer will be the receiver. The synthesizer will sound the note exactly as before, even though no key is being physically depressed.

One function of MIDI is to record musical performances. Another function is to synchronize several automatic devices, such as sequencers and drum machines, so that they are all perfectly in phase at all times.

One synthesizer could be set up as the sender, and a second synthesizer could be the receiver (slave). Sounds could be produced on the second synthesizer under the control of the first synthesizer's keyboard. In a sense, this gives the musician "extra hands."

Many other applications are also possible, of course, including;

- intelligent accompaniment systems
- intelligent arpeggiators
- multi-track polyphonic sequencers
- music transcriptions
- sound creation/ modification/ analysis

A general purpose "user-friendly" control language could be constructed from the basic MIDI commands. This would allow non-technically oriented users to create their own programs.

Multiple receivers and senders may be defined. Each MIDI signal is identified as belonging to a specific channel. A phrase sent to a device on channel 3 will be ignored by a device on channel 2. Each MIDI link can support up to 16 channels.

A single controlling device (sender), such as a microcomputer or master synthesizer, can be used to control several receivers.

Another advantage of the multi-channel capability is that it allows the MIDI user to take advantage of the multi-voice capabilities of many deluxe modern synthesizers.

Unfortunately, not all MIDI equipped devices are capable of sending or receiving data on multiple channels. This is especially true of synthesizers not designed for simultaneous independent voices, like the Korg Polysix, or the Sequential Circuits Prophet 5. These instruments have multiple voices, but all voices are programmed for a single sound. Therefore, only one MIDI channel is needed for full control of the instrument. Regrettably, this limits the possibilities of setting multiple similar synthesizers for independent control on different MIDI channels.

Since the channel definitions are software determined, they can easily be changed, even in the middle of a composition. This gives even greater versatility. In a sense, it is almost like having an infinite number of hardware channels available.

MIDI supports three different channel modes. They are:

OMNI
POLY
MONO

In the OMNI mode, the channel headings are ignored. The receiver accepts all incoming data, regardless of the channel assignments. This is the standard default mode. MIDI systems go directly into the OMNI mode at power-up.

The POLY mode uses the independent channels. Receiving devices will respond only to data with the appropriate channel heading.

The MONO mode is similar to the POLY mode, except only single note (monophonic) lines can be sent on each MIDI channel. The POLY mode allows full chords or polyphonic parts to be sent in a single channel, as long as all notes are to be sounded with a single voice. Why would you ever want the more limited MONO mode then? The MONO mode assigns each note event directly to a specific synthesizer voice, bypassing the normal internal note assignment algorithm. Another difference is that the MONO mode allows legato lines to be played. This is not possible in the POLY mode.

A MIDI channel can be programmed with several types of event data, selections followed by a number are further explained after the list:

- NOTE ON (1)
- NOTE OFF (1)
- PRESSURE/AFTER TOUCH (FOR INDIVIDUAL NOTES & OVERALL)
- PROGRAM CHANGES
- CONTROL CHANGES
    1 pitch bender
    channel MODE selector (2)
    32 ON/OFF switches
    3 primary controllers (3)
    28 secondary controls (3)
    29 "open" locations (4)
- CURRENT MEASURE NUMBER
- SONG SELECT (5)
- TUNE REQUEST (6)
- END OF BLOCK (7)

Some of these require a little explanation.

These define the begin and end points for individual notes. Velocity data may be optionally included.

This can also function as an "all notes off" command.

These controllers are undefined. That is, they are not bound to specific parameters. They may be programmed as needed. In addition, these are continuous controllers, similar to potentiometers (knobs). There are two resolution modes for each controller:

- Low resolution (128 possible values)
- High resolution (16,000 possible values)

Obviously, the low resolution mode will transfer data faster than the high resolution mode.

These are completely undefined at present. They are included to allow future expansion to the MIDI system.

Up to 128 different songs can be selected by number.

The TUNE REQUEST is used to instruct a connected unit (such as an expander module or slave synthesizer) to go through an internal "auto-tune" routine.

This is used to identify the end of System Exclusive information, including special function codes, or data for specific devices.

The MIDI software language also includes commands to program System Real Time Events. These are not channel specific.

- SYSTEM RESET CODE
- TIMING-CLOCK-IN-PLAY
- MEASURE END
- TIMING-CLOCK-IN-STOP
- START-FROM-FIRST-MEASURE
- CONTINUE-START

The SYSTEM RESET CODE initializes all devices in the system. It returns everything to the initial power-up condition.

The TIMING CLOCK puts out 24 steps per beat while the sender is in the PLAY mode. Only a single master clock should be active in the system. The MEASURE END signal is used in place of the ordinary CLOCK signal to signify the end of a measure. The CLOCK signal continues to function when the system is not in the PLAY mode. This keeps the various circuitry synchronized.

The START-FROM-FIRST-MEASURE is sent just before the first TIMING-CLOCK-IN-PLAY pulse when the master unit is put into the PLAY mode.

CONTINUE-START allows you to resume an interrupted musical passage, without going back to the first measure.

The MIDI commands are summarized in Table 4-1. Additional functions ("words") can be added to the MIDI software as needed. This makes the system theoretically obsolescence-proof.

New "instruments" can be created from devices with a major software component, just by changing the programming. Such customization and up-dating is not limited to the manufacturer. Users can write their own MIDI software. Modifications can be made to a MIDI synthesizer, without opening the case and voiding the warranty.

LIMITATIONS OF MIDI

MIDI software is not entirely an unmixed blessing, of course. The user buying a commercial program has no way of knowing if

Channel

The most significant four bits of each Channel status byte define the command while the least significant four bits identify the effective channel.

9xH   **NOTE ON EVENT**

3 bytes 1001 nnnn + 0kkk kkkk + 0vvv vvvv

> **nnnn**
> Channel code 0-15 corresponds to channel numbers 1-16
>
> **kkk kkkk**
> Key number 0-127
> For all keyboards, middle C = 60 All C key numbers are multiples of 12
> The standard five octave synth keyboard ranges 36-96
> The 88 note piano keyboard ranges 21-108
>
> **vvv vvvv**
> Key On velocity, 0-127
> With no velocity sensors, default to 64
> With velocity, 1 = ppp (softest), 127 = fff (loudest)
> Key On velocity = 0 turns note off

8xH   **NOTE OFF EVENT**

3 bytes 1000 nnnn + 0kkk kkkk + 0vvv vvvv

> **vvv vvvv**
> Key Off (release) velocity
> Implemented Prophet T8

AxH   **POLYPHONIC KEY PRESSURE**

3 bytes 1010 nnnn + 0kkk kkkk + 0vvv vvvv

> **vvv vvvv**
> Pressure/After-touch value 0-127
> Used in Omni mode (Compare code DxH Mono mode)

BxH   **CONTROL CHANGE**

3 bytes 1011 nnnn + 0ccc cccc + 0vvv vvvv

> **ccc cccc**
> Control address 0-127
> Except for the Pitch Bender (0), the controllers are not specifically defined. A manufacturer can assign the logical controllers to physical ones as necessary. The controller allocation table must be provided in the user's operation manual. Continuous controllers (including the Pitch bender) are divided into Most and Least Significant Bytes. If only 7

bits of resolution are needed for a specific controller, only the MSB is sent. It is not necessary to send the LSB. If more resolution is needed then both are sent first the MSB, then the LSB. If only the LSB has changed in value, the LSB may be sent without re-sending the MSB.

0	Pitch bender MSB
1	Controller 1 MSB
2	Controller 2 MSB
3	Controller 3 MSB
4-31	Continuous controllers 4-31 MSB
32	Pitch bender LSB
33	Controller 1 LSB
34	Controller 2 LSB
35	Controller 3 LSB
36-63	Continuous controllers 4-31 LSB
64-95	Switches (on/off)
96-123	Undefined
124	Local/Remote Keyboard Control (toggle)
125	Omni Mode Select/All notes off
126	Mono Mode Select/All notes off
127	Poly Mode Select/All notes off

If c = 125, 126, or 127, v (see below) must be 0

vvv vvvv
Control value, 0-127
For mode selections (c = 125, 126, or 127). vvv vvvv must be 0
Pitch benders should range from 0-127, with 64 being centre (no pitch bend).
Other controllers will range from 0 = minimum to 127 = maximum.
Switches are defined 0 = off, 127 = on

CxH   **PROGRAM CHANGE**

2 bytes: 1100nnnn + 0ppp pppp

ppp pppp
Program number, 0-127

DxH   **CHANNEL PRESSURE**

2 bytes: 1101nnnn + 0vvv vvvv

vvv vvvv
Channel pressure/after-touch amount, 0-127
For Mono mode: channel (rather than key) is identified.

ExH   **UNDEFINED**
(SCI uses this status for Pitch Wheel change in the Prophet-600)

46

System Exclusive

A format has been defined for System Exclusive information, consisting of a two byte preamble, the data itself, and a one-byte end code. The purpose of this format is to provide for the transmission of data which may be useful to any two instruments from one manufacturer but uninterpretable to other MIDI bussed devices. For example, SCI uses this protocol for loading and dumping program data. System Exclusive information can only be interrupted by a System Reset command.

Format F0H + 0iii iiii + data + F7H

F0H
Status byte. Must be followed by manufacturers ID#

0iii iiii
Manufacturers ID#
iii iiii can be 0-127
Current ID numbers are

Sequential Circuits	01H
Kawai	40H
Roland	41H
Korg	42H
Yamaha	43H

Receivers which do not recognize the ID# ignore the ensuing system exclusive data.

data
Any number of bytes
MSB must be reset (Otherwise will signal a new status byte). Data can range 0-127.
Data is intended for all channels.

F7H
An END-OF-BLOCK code which terminates System Exclusive status
SYSTEM RESET will also terminate System Exclusive status

In no case should other data or status codes be interleaved with System Exclusive data regardless of whether or not the ID code is recognized.

System Real Time

The System Real Time codes control the entire system in real time. They are used for synchronizing sequencers and rhythm units.
To maintain timing precision, these codes can be sent between any System Common or Channel data sets which consist of two or more bytes. However, the codes may not be interleaved with System Exclusive data.
System Real Time statuses are intended for all channels and recognized by all units using the interface. If the functions specified are not implemented, they are simply ignored.

F8H   TIMING-CLOCK-IN-PLAY
This clock is sent while the transmitter is in Play mode. The system is synchronized with this clock which is sent at a rate of 24 clocks/quarter note.

F9H	**MEASURE-END**

The MEASURE-END is transmitted instead of the TIMING-CLOCK-IN-PLAY at the end of of each measure.

FAH	**START-FROM-1ST-MEASURE**

This code is immediately sent when the play button on the master (e.g. sequencer or rhythm unit) is hit. The first TIMING-CLOCK-IN-PLAY must follow within 5 ms after this code.

FBH	**CONTINUE START**

This is sent when the CONTINUE button (on the master) is hit. A sequence will restart from the point where the sequence stopped on the last TIMING-CLOCK-IN-PLAY. The next TIMING-CLOCK-IN-PLAY be sent within 5 ms after this code.

FCH	**TIMING-CLOCK-IN-STOP**

This code is clocked in Stop mode to synchronize a Phase-Locked Loop (PLL) which is used (during Stop) for interpolating the timing clock.

System Common

System Common information is intended for all channels in a system.

F1H	**Undefined**

F2H	**MEASURE INFORMATION**

3 bytes F2H + 0mmm mmmm (MS) + 0mmm mmmm (LS)

The two data bytes code the 14-bit measure number.

F3H	**SONG SELECT**

2 bytes F3H + 0sss ssss

The data byte codes the 7-bit song number.

F4H	**Undefined**

F5H	**Undefined**

F6H	**TUNE REQUEST**

Initiates synthesizer tune routines

System Reset

There is one system reset code. It initializes the entire system to the condition of just having power switched on.

FFH	**SYSTEM RESET**

System Reset should be used sparingly, preferably under manual command only. In particular, it should not be sent automatically on power up. This could cause two units connected together to endlessly reset each other.

the software is any good or not. There are good programmers and bad programmers. Not all users are qualified (or inclined) to write their own software.

Unavoidably, the current MIDI standards aren't complete. New developments are bound to arise. The MIDI system has considerable leeway for adding new features, which is good, but different manufacturers might implement new features in different ways, creating various MIDI dialects which are only partially compatible. We can only hope that the efforts towards standardization continues. The manufacturers who use the MIDI system should periodically get together to update the standards to allow for new developments in a unified manner.

MIDI is not magical. Just because the MIDI system supports a given feature, that does not mean all MIDI compatible equipment can use it. MIDI is not implemented completely on all instruments. For example, many synthesizers can only function in the OMNI mode, even though the MIDI system supports two additional modes. Communication between MIDI devices can only occur at their lowest common level.

Updating older equipment to support MIDI is often impossible (without completely redesigning the equipment). Even when it is possible, it may be extremely impractical. In some cases a limited MIDI interface can be added, but compatibility with older, pre-MIDI instruments is not part of the MIDI standards.

The
5 SMPL Tape
Automation System

Synchronous Technologies (P.O. Box 14467, Oklahoma City, OK 73113) has developed a relatively low-cost high-tech automation system for tape recorder functions. The primary (but by no means only) market for this system is the one person studio, in which a single individual simultaneously serves as musician and engineer. Any one person has just two hands. An automated system like the SMPL can act as a well-trained assistant.

The SMPL system can be a major time-saver in the one person studio. In a multi-track composition you have to repeatedly return to the beginning of a specific section. Let SMPL do it. The automated punch-in/punch-out functions allow the user to concentrate on the actual engineering and/or performance, rather than concentrating to avoid missing the exact punch point.

TAPE HANDLING

Tape handling functions that can be turned over to the computer based SMPL system, shown in Fig. 5-1, include:

    auto-locate
    punch-in
    punch-out
    search-to-cue-point

and others.

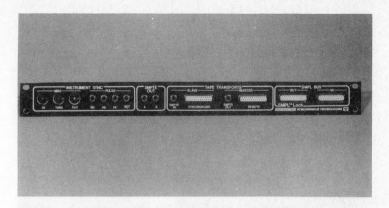

Fig. 5-1. Many tape handling functions can be turned over to the computer based SMPL system.

The SMPL computer is connected to the tape machine to be controlled via the recorder's remote control port. Obviously, a tape deck with remote control capability is required. Fortunately, such capability can be reasonably retro-fitted to most modern reel-to-reel tape decks.

SMPTE CODING

Thirty times a second, the SMPL system generates a SMPTE (Society of Motion Picture and Television Engineers) time code.

This time coding system is a standard in the audio/film/video industries. Each time code signal is a set of digital information uniquely identifying the current section of tape in hours, minutes, seconds, and frames. A frame is equal to 1/30 second. (This is the same as a video frame in standard television systems. Using the same base time period for both audio and video work is of obvious value.)

Currently the SMPL system isn't designed for machine-to-machine or audio/video synchronization, but these features may be included in future updates. There is nothing in the system to preclude such functions, they just aren't supported by the present version.

The first minute of the SMPTE time code during playback is treated as an "electronic leader." This electronic leader section is not intended to be part of the actual song or composition. As a result, SMPL differentiates between two distinct times:

TIME (total elapsed SMPTE time—including the electronic leader)
RUN TIME (total elapsed SMPTE time minus the one minute electronic leader)

Presumably, this is for the convenience of the computer system. The user must be careful not to get confused. Just remember, RUN TIME is always one minute behind TIME.

Each recorded track can be assigned its own individual eight digit "*slate*" *number*. Multiple takes of a single song can therefore be easily distinguished.

SYNCHRONIZED OUTPUTS

The SMPL also features a synchronized audible metronome output. The tape may be started at any point within a song, and SMPL's metronome will automatically synchronize itself to the song's tempo with milliseconds. There is no need to rewind the tape to the beginning of the song. The metronome will never be out of phase with the recorded tracks. The SMPL's metronome is programmable from 047 to 255 beats per minute.

The Sync output for driving drum machines or synchronizers (Garfield "Dr. Click," Oberheim DSX, PAIA "Master Synchronizer," etc.) can be set to 24, 48, or 96 pulses per quarter note. Most modern devices use one of these standards. The tape may be rolled from any point, and the sync output will automatically lock onto the metronome tempo and to any previously recorded tracks.

EVENTS

Eight programmable "events" can be set up on the SMPL. Generally these will be up to eight programmable auto-locate points, but optional accessories can be added to the system for programmable "events" like;

- channel mute
- channel pan
- EQ in
- EQ out

or similar on/off type functions.

DEFAULT VALUES

Some functions have specific default values, which will normally be assumed when the computer is turned on. The defaults are:

- 24 pulse per quarter note sync output signal.
- square wave sync output signal
- reel-to-reel recorder

These defaults can be changed simply by holding down one or more buttons when the computer is turned on. The button(s) is/are released when the display screen comes on.

To change the 24 pulses per quarter note to 48 pulses per quarter note, the CUE button is held in during power up. Alternatively, if 96 pulses per quarter note is preferred, the IN button is used.

To change the sync signal to a 0.5 ms pulse wave (instead of the normal square wave), the OUT button should be depressed when the computer is turned on.

The TRANSPORT button is held in during power up to tell the system that a cassette deck is being used instead of the normally assumed reel-to-reel deck.

THE REHEARSE PAGE

The SMPL computer is hooked up to any ordinary television

SMPTE	HR	MI	SE	FR
RUN TIM				
CUE				
RCRD IN				
RCRD OUT				
SLATE				
TIME	STOPPED			
NON-DROP		TAPE: > <		
TEMPO: 125		REHEARSE		
V 18 (C) 1984 JSS				

Fig. 5-2. Upon power-up the SMPL screen should look like this.

set to display system data. Upon power up, the screen should look like Fig. 5-2.

The display screen presents a single page at a time, but the SMPL system has four different pages, to display various aspects of the system's operation;

- REHEARSE
- ENTRY
- EVENT
- WRITE

The user can move from page to page with the ADVANCE and RETURN keys. Pressing ADVANCE moves the display one page forward. Pressing RETURN moves the display one page back.

Upon power-up, the REHEARSE page is displayed. We will explain the displayed items in the next few pages.

The first line is labelled SMPTE. This line simply identifies the units of measurement for the values appearing on lower lines. This line never changes. The units are as follows;

    HR = hours
    MI = minutes
    SE = seconds
    FR = frames

(Remember, 1 frame = 1/30th of a second.)

54

The next line is labelled RUN TIM, or run time. The initial one minute "electronic leader" (discussed earlier) is deleted from the time displayed here. The system run time is one minute less than the actual SMPTE time code being read from the tape. After the "leader" time has past, the RUN TIM line is updated for each frame (30 times a second).

The CUE line comes next. This one may seem a little complicated, because it serves somewhat different purposes at different times.

When the CUE button on the computer is pressed while the tape is rolling, the computer will store the RUN TIM value for later use, and displays this time value on the CUE line. Later, the SMPL system can be told to search-to-cue. It will automatically rewind or fast forward the tape deck (whichever is required) towards this point, stopping within 15 to 29 frames before the cue point.

SMPL stops a few milliseconds ahead of the actual cue point. The extra milliseconds are required for the computer to synchronize itself with the SMPTE time code track.

CUE also can indicate the starting point for the sync output. Once the cue point has been reached, the sync output begins generating a pulse signal with the first metronome beat. A drum machine or sequencer can be started precisely at the desired moment in perfect synchronization with the previously recorded track.

The next line is RCRD IN, or "record in." Pressing the IN button on the computer while the tape is rolling stores the current RUN TIME value in the computer memory and displays this time on the RCRD IN line. This time value is used for automatic punch-ins.

Similarly, the RCRDOUT or "record out," line displays the time for automatic punch-outs. This time value is stored by pressing the OUT button while the tape is running. The next line on the display is labelled SLATE. This line displays the unique eight-digit slate number used to specifically identify the recording.

The TIME line reads out the elapsed SMPTE time (the one minute electronic leader is not deleted) while the tape is running. The TIME line value will be one minute more than the RUN TIM value. If the tape is not running, this line will display the message STOPPED. If the tape is running but there is no recorded SMPTE time code, this line will read NO SYNC.

Below the TIME line are four boxes which display various status indications.

The Upper Left box indicates the type of SMPTE code being used. The default value is the Non-Drop Frame Format Time Code, which is displayed as NON-DROP.

The Upper Right box tells the user what mode the controlled tape transport is in. The following symbols are used:

> <	Stop
>	Play
. >	Record
> >	Fast Forward
< <	Rewind

The use of these symbols is pretty much self-explanatory.

Moving down, the Lower Left Box displays the tempo of the SMPL metronome. The default value is 125 beats per minute.

The Lower Right box identifies the current mode of operation. These operating modes will be described later in these chapters. For the time being, we will just list them:

ENTRY
EVENT
LOCATE
REHEARSE
TAKE
WRITE

The default mode is REHEARSE.

The last line on the display simply indicates the software version number and copyright date.

The REHEARSE mode is primarily intended to allow the user to practice a part before actually recording an overdub. The tape rolls as normal so you can hear previous parts (and the SMPL system can read the SMPTE timing data), and cue, as well as punch-in, and punch-out times can be set without the recorder actually switching into record. SMPL can produce a "beep" to let you know the punch-ins and punch-outs will occur at the proper times.

To actually record the overdub, the SMPL must be put into the TAKE mode by pressing the TAKE and TRANSPORT buttons. The REHEARSE display page remains on the screen.

A third mode, LOCATE, can also be entered directly from the REHEARSE mode, but the user does not have to be concerned with this mode. The computer will automatically enter this mode when performing search-to-cue functions.

THE ENTRY PAGE

The second page, obtained from the REHEARSE page by pressing the ADVANCE key once, is the ENTRY page. The display is the same as for the REHEARSE mode, but here the values are entered for the actual recording of overdubs, rather than rehearsal.

The cursor keys are used to select which line on the page you want to enter a value for. Number keys (1-0) are used to directly enter values into the CUE. RCRD IN, RECRDOUT, and TEMPO lines. Values may be carried over from the REHEARSE mode, or the REHEARSE values may be altered in the ENTRY mode.

All leading and trailing zeroes must be entered. For example, a time of 2 minutes, 50 seconds cannot be entered as 2:50. For the SMPL system to recognize the time value, it must be entered as 00:02:50:00. Similarly, a tempo of 85 BPM must be entered as 085.

The system will not allow you to enter an illegal value. For instance, if you tried to enter a tempo of 013, the cursor would automatically go back to the beginning of the TEMPO line so you can try again. If an illegal time (such as 73 in the minutes column) is entered, the system will not accept it, and the cursor will remain stationary.

THE EVENT PAGE

The next page (attained from the ENTRY mode by pressing the ADVANCE key once) is the EVENT page. The display for this page is illustrated in Fig. 5-3. The number keys (1-0) are used to enter up to eight separate event times. This time data is used for auto-locate, or to trigger events during tape playback.

THE WRITE PAGE

Pressing the ADVANCE key one more time brings you to the WRITE page. The display is the same as for the REHEARSE and ENTRY modes. The cursor is placed at the beginning of the SLATE line. The user then enters the eight digit identification (Slate) number.

GENERATING THE SMPTE CODE

Pressing the ADVANCE key one more time while on the

SMPTE	HR	MI	SE	FR
EVENT 1	0 0	0 0	0 0	0 0
EVENT 2	0 0	0 0	0 0	0 0
EVENT 3	0 0	0 0	0 0	0 0
EVENT 4	0 0	0 0	0 0	0 0
EVENT 5	0 0	0 0	0 0	0 0
EVENT 6	0 0	0 0	0 0	0 0
EVENT 7	0 0	0 0	0 0	0 0
EVENT 8	0 0	0 0	0 0	0 0
V18 (C) 1984 JSS				

Fig. 5-3. This is the display for the EVENT page.

WRITE page causes the system to start generating SMPTE time code. The value on the TIME line will be incremented 30 times a second (once per frame).

All keys, except for the RESTORE key, are "locked out" while the SMPL system is generating SMPTE time code. This prevents accidental interruption of the recording process. Pressing the RESTORE key stops the SMPTE time code, and returns the system to the REHEARSE mode. Conditions are now the same as at power-up, except the stored EVENT page times are not erased. To clear all functions (including the EVENT page), it is necessary to momentarily turn off the SMPL computer, then turn it back on again.

We have barely skimmed the surface of the SMPL system. Clearly, it can be a valuable assistant for any serious recording work, whether professional or hobbyist.

Part 2
Commercial Synthesizers

6
PAIA Kits

If money is tight or you enjoy building electronic projects, you might want to consider building your own custom-made synthesizer. This kind of approach is especially appropriate to the hobbyist, but of course, if enough care is exercised in construction, the end result could very well be a customized unit suitable for professional use.

PAIA Electronics produces an excellent series of kits for this purpose. Package systems are available, but they tend to be of the "one of each module" type, which very definitely limits their versatility. These packages aren't really supposed to be complete unto themselves as much as merely a starting point for a customized system. Since you're building the whole thing yourself anyway, it's easy enough to add on whatever modules you might want. And you don't have to pay for anything you don't need either.

The manuals are clearly written and no one with just the slightest bit of soldering experience should run into any major difficulties building the kits. If you're an absolute novice with a soldering iron, practice on some cheap kit first. Radio Shack carries a series of beginner kits for under $10. You probably won't be able to find anything for your synthesizer, but you just want something to practice on, so an extra AM radio won't really hurt.

There is one point about construction that I differ with PAIA on rather strongly: the use of sockets for the integrated circuits. PAIA holds that IC sockets are wasteful—often costing more than the IC itself—and make it easy to install the IC backwards, which would probably destroy it the instant power is applied. Frankly, I've found it just as easy to solder in an IC backwards. Carelessness is carelessness with or without sockets (and we all do it once in a while). If you're careful, it should not happen in either case. But sometimes it does. And sometimes you apply a little too much heat when soldering and burn out the IC. And frequently (more often than you might like to think) the IC is simply a dud in the first place. If any of these things happen and you have to desolder an IC and install a new one, you're certain to wish you'd gone to the expense of using a socket. IC sockets aren't too terribly expensive considering the frustrating waste of time they can prevent, especially if you get a pack of a dozen or so. If you're building an entire synthesizer, you'll probably use all of them sooner or later. As it turns out, though, this series of kits really doesn't use many ICs.

PAIA offers two VCO modules. The less expensive of the pair has a range from 20 Hz to 5000 Hz. This is the fundamental frequency only, of course—the harmonics go much higher. This module has three outputs—ramp or sawtooth, triangle and pulse waves. There is a manual control to adjust the pulse width. A separate module does it with voltage control, which can also convert a triangle wave into a sine wave. This VCO has three frequency modulation control voltage inputs.

The deluxe, wide-range VCO costs about $10 more and offers a frequency range that extends from 16 Hz to 16 kHz, along with simultaneously available ramp, triangle, sine and variable-width pulse wave outputs. The pulse width on this VCO can be voltage controlled without a separate converter module. This kit also has an initial pitch control to tune more than one VCO to a constant relationship with each other for constant-form chords or whatever.

Three VCFs are offered by PAIA: a low-pass, a band-pass, and a deluxe multimodel module that has simultaneous low-pass and band-pass outputs. An inverter is also available to convert the low-pass filter to a high-pass, and the band-pass to a band-reject, or notch filter via phase cancellation. The inverter can also be used to increase the Q of the lower priced filters. The multimodel VCF has adjustable Q available as a front panel control.

PAIA also makes two envelope generator kits. The simpler of the two has control for attack and decay. Sustain will be held as long as the trigger signal is present (the key is held down, for instance). There is an OUTPUT LEVEL on this module that effectively acts as a SUSTAIN LEVEL control, so all that is really missing is the initial decay.

The more complex envelope generator is of the full ADSR type. There are controls for attack time, initial decay time, sustain level and final release time, as well as an overall OUTPUT LEVEL control that determines how high the attack voltage will go.

Another useful module is the control oscillator/noise source, which is essentially two modules in one. The noise source has only an output jack on the front panel and so few components that it would seem wasteful to devote an entire module just to it.

The control oscillator produces a sinewave output from 1 Hz to 25 Hz in three switch-selectable ranges. There is also an OUTPUT LEVEL control for the control oscillator section. This module is generally used for such effects as tremolo and vibrato.

PAIA also carries kits for a VCA, a ring (balanced) modulator, a stereo mixer and a sequencer, along with such essential things as power supplies. There is also a module kit called the Envelope Follower/Trigger that allows you to interface other instruments with your synthesizer.

If you want an even simpler and less expensive synthesizer, take a look at PAIA's Gnome microsynthesizer kit. This is a small, hand-held unit, about the size of a lunch box. It has a VCO, a VCF, a VCA, a noise source and a ribbon controller. The VCF and VCA each have their own independent envelope generators.

The VCO is unique. It has triangle and square wave outputs that can be used simultaneously with different output levels. There is also a control labeled SKEW. This SKEW control acts as a variable-pulse width control for the square wave, and allows the triangle wave to be continuously variable from a clean, sharp triangle to an ascending sawtooth wave. Some of the in-between settings of this control are very unique and extremely interesting.

All of the interconnections of the Gnome are normalized, and the normalization scheme is shown in Fig. 2-1.

Another PAIA kit of interest is the Proteus I lead synthesizer. It is basically a normalized analog synthesizer with a built-in 3 octave keyboard. It is designed around the Curtis Electro-music ICs.

The various sound parameters in the Proteus I can be varied over a fairly wide range. The VCOs and VCF cover a 12 octave range. The LFO can be set for frequencies ranging from 0.066 Hz. to 15 Hz. Envelope parameters (ATTACK and DECAY/RELEASE times) range from 1 ms (0.001 second) to 30 seconds.

A number of jacks on the back of the instrument allow the user to bypass the normalization hook-ups for maximum flexibility.

The Proteus I has a computer interface, but it is not MIDI compatible. The kit is currently priced at $500.

PAIA also makes an organ kit (ORGANTUA), which is essentially an organ/synthesizer hybrid. Another popular kit from PAIA is STRINGZ 'N' THINGZ, a string synthesizer/electric piano. Both of these kits sell for $400 each.

PAIA makes a number of additional sound synthesis kits including a drum synthesizer, a programmable automatic drummer, a phlanger, a limiter, a reverb unit, an equalizer, and many others. Their address is 1020 W. Wilshire, Oklahoma City, OK 73116.

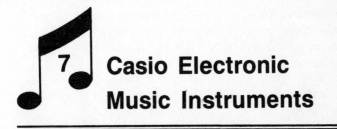

7 Casio Electronic Music Instruments

Casio (15 Gardner Rd, Fairfield, NJ 07006) manufactures several miniature electronic musical instruments. The low end of their line are essentially toys, but some of their deluxe models are up to near-professional standards. Many of these instruments are not quite synthesizers in the usual sense, but they certainly aren't organs either. Whatever they are, they are of interest to the electronic musician.

THE MZ-101 AND CZ-101 MINI-KEYBOARD

The Casio MZ-101 mini-keyboard covers a 4 octave range (C to C, 49 keys). Miniature keys are used on this compact MIDI compatible instrument. The white keys are 3¼″ deep. The MZ-101 is unquestionably portable, weighing a mere 7¼ pounds. It is only 26″ wide by 2½″ high by 8¼″ deep. Many would consider the reduced size keyboard a reasonable trade-off for the convenience of slinging this light-weight instrument right under your arm, and easily carrying it wherever you want to go.

Up to eight single oscillator voices may be set up on this instrument. Alternatively, four double-oscillator voices may be defined. Three eight-stage envelopes are provided for each oscillator, permitting a large variety of possibilities.

Sixteen factory preset voices are included in memory. In addition, the musician may program sixteen voice patches of his own. External cartridges can be used to load sixteen additional voices. A multi-segment LCD panel displays programmed patch data. Values for various parameters of each voice are selected via a pair of simple up/down buttons.

A single oscillator voice on the CZ-101 consists of an oscillator, an amplifier and three eight-stage envelope generators (pitch, waveform, and amplitude). Eight basic waveforms are available. A total of 33 different waveforms can be created by combing the basic waveforms in pairs within a single oscillator.

Independent rate and level settings can be defined for each stage of each envelope. Any of the eight stages can be defined as a sustain. Some pretty wild envelopes can be set up using this system, as illustrated in Fig. 7-1. Clearly, a great many interesting voices can be set up on this instrument.

Even more voices can be created by blending two oscillator channels into a single voice. A line select control is provided with four settings;

$$1$$
$$2$$
$$1 + 2'$$
$$1 + 1'$$

The first two, of course, are basic single oscillator voices. The second two options are doubled voices. The mark after the second line number in these voices indicate that this oscillator channel is detuned. The amount of detuning is fully adjustable.

Other features of the CZ-101 include;

automatic transposition
compare button (for ABing edited patches)
phase distortion

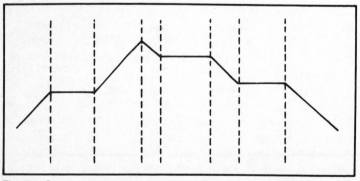

Fig. 7-1. Some pretty wild envelopes can be set up on the MZ-10.

66

pitch-bend wheel (variable range)
portamento
ring modulation
tone mixing (layering two two-oscillator voices on top of one another)
vibrato (variable waveshape, rate, depth, and delay)

The basic functions of this instrument are simple enough for the beginner or hobbyist to quickly learn. On the other hand, it has many powerful capabilities that would be valuable to the professional musician. Casio seems to attempt to provide something for everybody in their products. The current retail price for the CZ-101 is $500.

The CZ-1000 ($700) is similar, except it has a standard, full-size keyboard.

THE CT-610

Another Casio instrument is the CT-610, which features 24 accompaniment variations, and 12 auto-rhythms. Twenty preset sounds are available. The full-size keyboard covers a 5 octave range (61 keys). This is a semi-polyphonic keyboard. Up to 8 notes may be simultaneously sounded.

The CT-610 has built-in stereophonic speakers. A number of jacks are provided to add auxiliary equipment. The CT-610 currently retails for about $700.

The CT-7000 AND CT-6000

Casio's CT-7000 is designed to take advantage of digital capabilities. It has a built-in memory system which can function as a multi-track recorder. Two prerecorded parts may be played back at the same time. Accompanying chords may also be stored in the special chord channel. Two special effect channels are also available to add subtle nuances to recorded sequences.

This instrument is designed for stereophonic operation, but it is more than just straight two-channel sound. The SLS (Sound Locating System) allows you to position the sound in any of 7 different locations throughout the stereo field. Sounds can be made to move smoothly from speaker to speaker.

The CT-7000 also features 20 preset sounds, auto-accompaniment, and 12 auto-rhythms. Special effects available include sustain, vibrato, and delayed vibrato.

The full-size 61 key (5 octave) keyboard is 8 note polyphonic. A pitch control is provided to tune the instrument.

A LCD is used to read out music data. Recorded sequences can be saved on a cassette tape via the built-in tape recorder interface. Several input and output jacks are provided to allow convenient expansion to the system. This instrument is priced at $1000.

Priced at about $1000 is the CT-6000. The full-size 61 key (5 octave) keyboard is touch sensitive, allowing greater expressiveness. In addition, the automatic accompaniment responds to the player's pressure variations.

The 20 preset voices include;

brass ensemble
jazz organ
reed
synth
piano
electric piano
harpsichord
pipe organ
trumpet
violin
flute and others

A tone-mix option is offered. This allows the user to create individual sounds by blending a melody tone with a different accompaniment tone.

The auto-accompaniment operates in three modes;

easy "Casio Chord"
normal "Fingered"
high-level "Free Bass Chord"

In addition, the chord memory can store up to 100 chords for later playback.

Twelve automatic rhythm patterns are also provided. These include;

bossa nova
disco
march
reggae

rock
samba
swing
waltz

The CT-6000 also features three unison effects and five sound effects. It includes a pitch bender for portamento type effects. This instrument is MIDI compatible.

OTHER CASIO INSTRUMENTS

Casio also manufactures a number of simpler electronic musical instruments. These are designed primarily for the amateur. They are good learning machines, and offer several interesting preset voices.

Most current models also feature automatic accompaniment features.

Since these devices aren't really intended for serious musicians, we won't go into great depth. However, thanks to their convenient portability, they can come in handy for practice, and other non-critical applications. They can be a good, low-cost second instrument.

The PT-1 ($50)

29 keys (monophonic)
4 preset sounds
10 auto-rhythms
tempo control
melody storage
auto-play
one key play

The PT-31 (price unavailable)

31 keys
7 preset sounds
18 auto-rhythms
tempo control
auto-accompaniment
automatic chord harmonize
melody storage
auto-play
one key play
save and load on cassette tape

The CK-10 ($80)

   29 keys (monophonic)
   4 preset sounds
   10 auto-rhythms
   melody storage
   auto-play
   one key play
   built-in AM/FM radio
   built-in stereo speakers

The PT-80 ($100)

   32 keys
   8 preset sounds
   12 auto-rhythms
   in tempo guide
   melody guide
   cancel guide
   auto-play
   one key play
   prerecorded ROM packs available

The MT-35 ($130)

   44 keys
   6 preset sounds
   4 auto-rhythms
   8 note polyphonic
   auto accompaniment
   pitch control

The MT-36 ($130)

   similar to the MT-35

The MT-46 ($170)

   49 keys
   8 preset sounds
   8 auto-rhythms
   Casio chord

manual bass
sound effects
vibrato
sustain

The MT-200 ($200)

49 keys
8 preset sounds
6 auto-rhythms
8 note polyphonic
auto accompaniment
pitch control
built-in stereo speakers

The MT-100 ($200)

49 keys
20 preset sounds
12 auto-rhythms
8 note polyphonic
4 types of bass & chord selectors
auto-accompaniment
pitch control
graphic equalizer
sound effects
vibrato
delayed vibrato
sustain
reverb

The MT-210 ($250)

49 keys
20 preset sounds
12 auto-rhythms
8 note polyphonic
4 types of bass & chord selectors
auto-accompaniment
pitch control
built-in stereophonic speakers
sound effects

vibrato
delayed vibrato
stereo chorus
reverb
Pulse Code Modulation sound generator for dynamic drum
sounds

The MT-85 ($300)

49 keys
12 preset sounds
12 auto-rhythms
8 note polyphonic
auto-play
one-key chords
Casio chord
manual memory
prerecorded ROM packs available
sound effects
sustain
stereo chorus

The CT-310 ($300)

49 keys (full size)
12 preset sounds
12 auto-rhythms
8 note polyphonic
auto-accompaniment (up to 768 variations)
pitch control
4 types of bass & chord selectors

The MT-800 ($500)

49 keys
12 preset sounds
12 auto-rhythms
8 note polyphonic
auto-play
one-key chords
Casio chord
manual memory

prerecorded ROM packs available
detachable stereo speakers

The MT-810 ($700)

49 keys (full size)
12 preset sounds
12 auto-rhythms
8 note polyphonic
auto-play
one-key chords
Casio chord
manual memory
prerecorded ROM packs available
built-in stereo speakers

The MT-400V ($400)

49 keys
20 preset sounds
12 auto-rhythms
8 note polyphonic
auto-accompaniment (192 variations)
detachable stereo speakers
sound effects
reverb
stereo chorus
sustain
vibrato

The CT-410V ($500)

49 keys (full size)
20 preset sounds
12 auto-rhythms
8 note polyphonic
auto-accompaniment (192 variations)
built-in stereo speakers
sound effects
reverb
stereo chorus
sustain

vibrato
delayed vibrato

Clearly Casio offers a wide range of choices for almost anyone from the beginning hobbyist to the professional musician looking for a second instrument.

8

Siel Synthesizers

Music Technology, Inc. (105 Fifth Ave., Garden City Park, N.Y. 11040) markets a line of analog and digital synthesizer equipment under the Siel name.

THE OR400 ENSEMBLE ANALOG POLY SYNTHESIZER

Siel's OR400 is an analog type polyphonic synthesizer. It's control panel is made up of 9 push buttons and 32 slider controls.

One nice feature is a patch diagram drawn directly on the control panel, as shown in Fig. 8-1. Other manufacturers of normalized (no patch cords or pins) analog synthesizers should consider following Siel's lead here. Surely printing such a diagram on the control panel doesn't cost very much, but it can be very helpful, especially to the beginner learning how to operate the instrument.

In our discussion we will move across the control panel from left to right. The first slider control is for pitch bend/keyboard transposition. A small push button over this slider determines if the pitch will be flat or sharp.

Next comes a 5 stage graphic equalizer. A push button switches the equalizer in or out of the circuit. Five slider controls adjust the following frequencies;

250 Hz.
500 Hz.

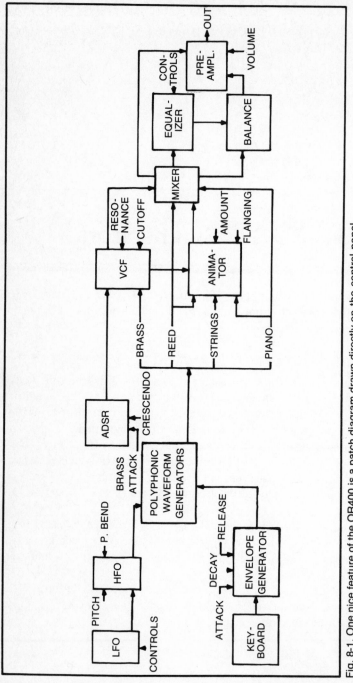

Fig. 8-1. One nice feature of the OR400 is a patch diagram drawn directly on the control panel.

1000 Hz.
2000 Hz.
4000 Hz.

A sixth slider control is labelled BALANCE. This control sets the relative levels of the direct and equalized signals. This allows the musician to fade the equalization in or out of the sound, and to control the overall depth of the filtering effects.

A slider control to adjust the main volume of the entire instrument comes next. Beneath the volume control is a push button for dropping the pitch down an octave.

The next section is called the Animator, which serves as a modulator. A push button switch turns the effect on and off. Two slider controls are labelled AMOUNT and FLANG. (Flanging).

Another push button switch turns the LFO on and off. Three slider controls are associated with the LFO;

SPEED (frequency)
DEPTH
DELAY

The remainder of the controls on the OR400 are for the various presets. Four preset buttons are provided;

BRASS
PIANO
REED
STRINGS

A number of slider controls are associated with each of these presets. For example, in the BRASS section we find;

ATTACK
CUTOFF
TROMBONE
CRESCENDO
RESONANCE

The PIANO section consists of;

DECAY
PIANO

CLAVICHORD
HONKY TONK

There are three controls in the REED section;

CHURCH ORGAN
ACCORDIAN
MUSETTE

Finally, in the STRINGS section, we have the following controls;

ATTACK
RELEASE
CELLO
VIOLIN
MUTE
PERCUSSION

Each of the four presets can produce a number of different voices. This is an interesting compromise between straight patch, and direct preset synthesis. The OR400 is currently priced at $600.

THE PX JR.

The PX Jr. (also a SIEL instrument) is a fully polyphonic preset synthesizer with dynamic touch sensitivity, which the manufacturer claims is similar to that of a traditional acoustic piano.

This is a very easy to use preset-type instrument. Very few user controls are provided. There are five basic presets;

PIANO 1
PIANO 2
ELECTRIC PIANO
HARPSICHORD
HONKY TONK

No provisions are made for the user to create his own voices, although the presets may be enhanced with a variable speed stereophonic CHORUS effect. A Sustain pedal is also provided.

The PX Jr. features a built-in 9 watt (RMS) amplifier and loudspeaker. It also has a pair of stereo outputs for driving external amplifiers or headphones. This 72 key instrument is currently priced just under $600.

THE MK900 PRESET PIANO KEYBOARD

Another instrument in the SIEL line is the MK900, priced at $700. This instrument is MIDI compatible.

Ten presets are provided. Each with two sound generations, giving a rich, spacious sound. A sound can be layered over itself, or two sounds may be combined.

The five octave (61 key) keyboard may be split to separate two different sounds, or allow up to 16 keys to play with one timbre.

The MK900 features Auto-Accompaniment with multiple modes. Several built-in rhythms may be used, or original patterns may be recorded.

A built-in 450 note sequencer is also included. This sequencer features battery back-up, so sequences are not lost during transportation or storage of the instrument.

Additional features of the SIEL MK900 include;

- built-in speakers
- chorus
- stereo detune
- transpose

THE DK600
PROGRAMMABLE POLYPHONIC SYNTHESIZER

SIEL's deluxe offering is the DK600 programmable polyphonic synthesizer, which has a price tag just under $1300, and is MIDI compatible.

The DK600 features 12 DCOs (Digitally Controlled Oscillators)—two each for six voices. These DCOs offer excellent pitch stability without any special tuning. Three LFOs (Low Frequency Oscillators) are also included for a wide variety of modulation effects.

A programmable dynamic envelope generator is also provided. The user can control both the parameter times and the ADSR destination. The envelope can be applied to the filter, the amplifier, or both.

The control panel is laid out to give an immediate visual indication of the operation of the current program. All selectors are provided with LED indicators. In addition, simple real-time adjustments can be made on all sound parameters. The memory contains 95 programs. The DK600 also has a cassette interface for long term storage.

An Expander unit ($800) is also available to extend the capabilities of the DK600 or other MIDI equipped synthesizer. In essence, the Expander adds an additional programmable, 6 voice, polyphonic MIDI synthesizer to your system, operated from a previously existing keyboard, or sequencer.

Like the DK600, the Expander's voices are made up of pairs of DCOs. This unit also features;

- 3 LFOs
- 6 low-pass filters (24 dB/octave)
- 6 envelope generators
- 95 factory programs

The MIDI interface allows such functions as;

- compatibility with other MIDI equipped instruments, sequencers, and microcomputers
- direct control of program parameters from a master keyboard or other MIDI equipped device
- direct loading of programs from a master keyboard or other MIDI equipped device
- linking to another MIDI equipped keyboard

SIEL's Expander also features a cassette interface for external storage of programs.

Push-button controls are provided, which can change sound parameters in real-time. The frequency of the DCOs is potentiometer controlled.

The Expander allows the keyboard to be split at any point, playing two simultaneous voices. One program (one section of the keyboard) is set up on the master synthesizer, while the Expander provides the second voice.

You can even simultaneously use two or more Expanders in the MIDI-POLYMODE. Data can be individually encoded for each independent Expander unit.

MIDI COMPUTER INTERFACE

SIEL also makes a more or less universal MIDI computer interface for connecting MIDI equipped instruments with many popular microcomputers, using the following CPUs;

6502
6510
Z80

A partial list of compatible microcomputers includes;

APPLE II
Commodore CBM64
Sinclair ZX Spectrum
Sinclair ZX81
TRS-80
VIC20

and a considerable number of others.

Bivalent connectors are provided for the Commodore CBM64 and the Sinclair ZX Spectrum. SIEL's MIDI Computer Interface runs about $150.

9

The Emulator

The Emulator from E-Mu Systems, Inc. (2815 Chanticleer, Santa Cruz, CA 95062) was one of the first major digital synthesizers. This instrument is based on digital sampling. Any sound can be recorded on a floppy disk, and played across the entire range of the keyboard. Besides mimicking any traditional musical instrument, the Emulator allows the musician to play music on voices based on dripping water, squeaky sneakers, a bouncing basketball, a banged garbage can lid, or whatever. If you an hear it, the Emulator can sample and manipulate it.

A few years ago, an updated model, the Emulator II was released. As with the earlier version, any sound can be recorded and played back polyphonically via the 61 key (5 octave) keyboard. The keyboard is velocity sensitive to permit expressive control of several sound parameters. The dynamic response of the instrument can be programmed to match the playing style of the individual musician.

The sound quality of the Emulator II has been significantly improved. The playback frequency range covers the complete audible spectrum (20 Hz to 20,000 Hz). The dynamic range of this instrument is rated at 96 dB—better than most high fidelity stereo systems. Sampled sounds can be up to 17 seconds long. A floppy disk can hold up to a megabyte of sampling data.

The recorded sounds can be manipulated with a number of

synthesizer module functions. The Emulator II features VCFs, VCAs, envelope generators, and independent LFOs for each of its eight channels. A recorded sound can be subtly altered, or it can be rendered completely unrecognizable with these functions.

The Emulator II also features digital editing functions, such as splicing and merging. Part of one sound can be combined with part of a second sound to create a new sound. For example, you could set up a voice with the attack of a flute, and the decay of a guitar.

Another unique effect available on the Emulator II is dynamic crossfading between voices via the keyboard velocity sensor. If a key is partially depressed, voice A will be heard. As the key is depressed further it will fade into voice B.

CONTROL PANEL

The control panel is divided into 10 sections. The controls available on the Emulator II are as follows.

MASTER CONTROL SECTION
   Keypad (select preset/ select menu function/ enter data)
   Mix output volume
   Select dynamic allocation
   Sliders A - D (set parameters)
   Transpose keyboard
   Tune keyboard

FILTER SECTION
   Envelope modulation amount
   Filter ADSR parameters (envelope)
   Frequency
   LFO modulation depth
   Keyboard tracking
   Resonance

VCA/LFO SECTION
   LFO delay
   LFO modulation depth (VCA)
   LFO random variation
   LFO rate (frequency)
   VCA ADSR parameters (envelope)

VOICE DEFINITION SECTION

Backwards mode
Bidirectional looping
Display sound length (bytes)
Digitally combine voices
Loop in release
Realtime control enable
Save voice to disk
Solo mode
Sound splicing
Velocity control designations:
  VCA attack
  VCA level
  VCF attack
  VCF frequency
  VCF resonance
Vibrato depth
Voice level
Voice looping
Voice truncation
Voice tuning

PRESET DEFINITION SECTION

Arpeggiator parameters
Assign voice to keyboard
Catalog presets in bank
Catalog sequences in bank
Catalog voice in bank
Copy/rename preset
Copy/rename voice
Create positional crossfade
Create preset
Create velocity crossfade
Create velocity switch
Deassign voice from keyboard
Display memory remaining
Edit voice assignment
Erase bank from memory
Erase preset from memory
Erase sequence from memory
Erase voice from memory
Get voice from disk

MIDI parameters
Nontransposition mode
Replicate preset

REALTIME CONTROLS SECTION
Continuous control sources:
Footpedal
Left wheel
Right wheel
MIDI controls A,B,C
Destinations:
Pitch
Filter Fc
Level
LFO > pitch
LFO > Fc
LFO > level
ADSR attack rate
Switch control sources:
Footswitches 1 and 2

DESTINATIONS:
Advance preset
Release
Sample
Sequencer control
Sustain
Sustenuto

DISK SECTION
Catalog voices
Copy disk
Disk space remaining
Erase voice from disk
Format disk
Get bank from disk 1
Get bank from disk 2
Save bank to disk

SPECIAL SECTION
Catalog current special functions

SEQUENCER SECTION
Define:
    Create sequence
    Set sequence length
    Set time signature
Edit:
    Append sequence
    Bounce tracks
    Erase track
    Punch in
    Reassign preset
    Store controls
External clock
Play
Record
Select sequence
Setup:
    Select cue tracks
    Select track
    Set autocorrect
    Set countdown
    Set SMPTE start
    Set tempo
Stop

SAMPLE SECTION
Arm sampling
Define voice
Force sampling
Gain set
Sample length
Stop sampling
Threshold set
VU display

AVAILABLE VOICES

Many predesigned voices are available directly from E-mu Systems. Here are some examples of currently available sound disks:

Accordian/ Banjo
Acoustic Guitar
Arco Bass/ Cello/ Violas

Armageddon
Assorted Trombones
Base Clarinet/ Clarinet
Bassoon/ Flute
Bass/ Synthesizer/ Drums
Digital Synth
Electric Guitar/ Mutes/ Harmonics
Electric Piano
Funk/ Rock Bass Guitar
Gong/ Tympani/ Voices
Grand Piano
Grand Piano/ Strings
Harp
Harpsichord
Kalimba/ Shaku-hachi
Lead Guitar
Marcato Strings
Nylon Guitar/ Mandolin
Orchestral Tune
Percussion
Rock Organs
Solo Cello/ Solo Violin
Stacked Strings
Tremolonde Bass/ Violas
Trumpet/ Trombone/ Sax/ French Horn
Vibes/ Marimba
Wind Chimes/ Birds/ Stream

New voice disks are continuously being released. The user can also make his own custom samples.

OTHER FEATURES

As with the majority of digital synthesizers today, the Emulator II is MIDI compatible. It has a powerful MIDI sequencer with features such as extensive editing functions, and automatic correction.

There is also a SMPTE reader/generator built into the instrument. It conforms to the synchronization standards used professionally in recording studios (including film and video).

A RS-422 interface is provided for computer control. This instrument is also expandable. Current and future options include:

"Digidesign" for coupling the Emulator II with a Macintosh computer

Hard disk for greatly increased storage capabilities

SMPTE based event oriented sequencer for creating automated sound effects tracks.

The base price for a single disk Emulator II is about $8000. A dual disk system runs about $8650. Of course prices are subject to change.

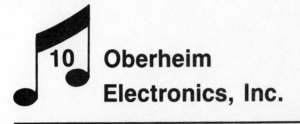

10 Oberheim Electronics, Inc.

Oberheim Electronics, Inc. (2250 S. Barrington Ave., Los Angeles, CA 90064) is one of the old-timers of the electronic music synthesizer industry. It is one of the relatively few companies that successfully made a blend of traditional analog instruments and modern digital devices.

THE OB-8 PROGRAMMABLE POLYPHONIC SYNTHESIZER

Maximum programmability was clearly a major design objective for Oberheim's OB-8. This powerful MIDI equipped synthesizer, shown in Fig. 10-1, has a full size 5 octave, polyphonic keyboard. Eight synthesizer voices can be set up directly from the front panel. Each voice is made up of;

- 2 oscillators
- 1 selectable 2 pole/4 pole filter
- 2 ADSR envelope generators
- 1 VCA

Each oscillator may be programmed for pulse, sawtooth, and triangle waves. Simultaneous sawtooth and pulse waves are also possible. The pulse width is programmable for both oscillators. The two oscillators may be synchronized together, if desired. Other

Fig. 10-1. The OB-8 is a powerful MIDI equipped synthesizer from Oberheim.

interesting timbres can be created by frequency modulating with the filter envelope.

Up to 120 voices can be stored in the OB-8's program memory. The instrument is supplied with 104 factory programmed voices. Even more voices can be stored externally via the built-in cassette interface.

Up to 12 split patch combinations can also be memorized by the OB-8. The keyboard split point and the audio balance between the two patches can be easily stored along with the upper and lower patches and their transpositions. In addition 12 double combinations can be stored to produce two distinct sounds with each keyboard depression.

Many different modulation effects can be created with the OB-8's LFOs (Low Frequency Oscillators). A large number of parameters are controllable from the front panel. Available LFO outputs include;

- negative sawtooth wave
- positive sawtooth wave
- square wave
- triangle wave
- sample and hold

All LFO waveforms may be retriggered from the keyboard.

The LFO modulation signal can be routed to any or all of the following destinations;

- VCO 1 frequency
- VCO 2 frequency
- VCO 1 pulse width
- VCO 2 pulse width
- filter frequency
- VCA

In the PAGE 2 mode (described later in this section) even greater control is provided over the modulation effects. LFO phase may be offset for rich, deep ensemble patches, or for lively stereo movement.

Attack and delay can be added to each of the LFO modulation busses. The delay control can be inverted. The modulation rate (LFO frequency) can be controlled via the keyboard, or the delay envelope. Clearly, the range of possible modulation effects isn't very limited on the OB-8.

The PAGE 2 mode assigns secondary functions to over half of the OB-8's front panel controls. Some of the new functions have already been mentioned. Other PAGE 2 capabilities include programmable portamento (you can select anything from a smooth glide to quantized portamento that moves chromatically) and control over the sustain footswitch release for each patch.

The OB-8 features an automatic arpeggiator. The individual notes of a chord may be arpeggiated in the order they were first played, or reverse order, or forwards then backwards, or in random order with emphasis on the lowest note of the chord. Basically an analog synthesizer, the OB-8 is MIDI compatible.

MATRIX-12 PROGRAMMABLE
MIDI KEYBOARD SYNTHESIZER

The top of Oberheim's line is the Matrix-12, shown in Fig. 10-2. The company claims this twelve voice instrument is the ultimate analog synthesizer, and there is certainly plenty to support this claim.

Even though the Matrix-12 is an analog synthesizer, it makes considerable use of modern digital technology, and has a very sophisticated MIDI interface.

The full size five octave keyboard is polyphonic and velocity sensitive. The velocity scale is selectable to tailor the keyboard's response to the musician's playing style. The keyboard responds to after-touch pressure as well as attack and release velocity. A unique feature of the Matrix-12 (one of many) is that these velocity signals can control virtually any parameter of each voice, including;

- detune
- envelope times
- filter frequency
- filter resonance
- FM amount
- lag
- LFO rate
- vibrato
- volume

This instrument undeniably places quite a bit of modulation control literally at the musician's fingertips.

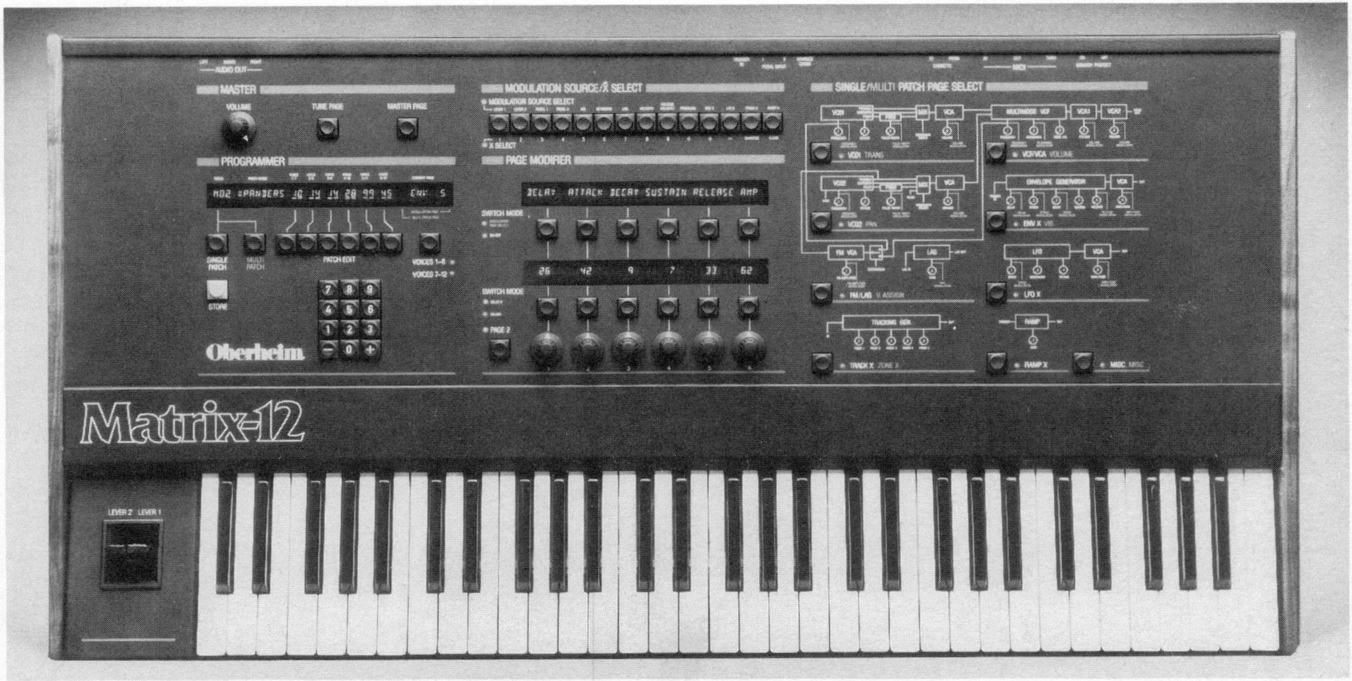

Fig. 10-2. The top of Oberheim's line is the MATRIX-12.

The Matrix-12's keyboard can be split into six overlapping sections (Zones) of two voices each. All twelve voices are individually programmable and may each have an entirely different sound.

Zones may be controlled from other MIDI devices, with or without a section of the Matrix-12's keyboard. This instrument is a good choice as a master controller in a multi-instrument MIDI system. Here's just one possibility;

- ZONES 1, 2, and 3 controlled by the MATRIX-12's own keyboard
- ZONE 4 controlled by external sequencer #1
- ZONE 5 controlled by external sequencer #2
- ZONE 6 controlled by an external synthesizer keyboard

The Matrix-12 can simultaneously produce all the voices for these various parts. All this complexity can be stored in one of the 100 Multi-Patches and recalled at the touch of a button.

This instrument is actually an analog/digital hybrid. Many analog functions are simulated digitally, but behave as if they were performed by dedicated analog circuitry.

Each of the twelve voices on the Matrix-12 are made up of the following stages;

- 2 VCOs with variable pulse, sawtooth, and triangle waves available on both
- 15 mode filter
- 5 ADSR envelope generators with initial delay and several programmable triggering modes
- 4 ramp generators, each with programmable ramp rate and several triggering modes
- 5 LFOs with Negative Sawtooth, Positive Sawtooth, Square, Triangle, Random, and Noise waveforms, sampling of any modulation source and several programmable triggering modes
- 3 tracking generators to alter the scaling or shape of a modulation source
- lag processor for Portamento effects of any modulation source
- FM VCA for Dynamic Linear Frequency modulation of VCO1 or the filter by VCO2
- 2 output amplifiers in series with programmable stereo panning

There are a total of 27 modulation sources for each voice, and 47 potential destinations for each of these modulation sources.

Clearly the number of voices and variations available on this machine is staggeringly large.

A 120 character flourescent alphanumeric display reads out programmed data on each patch and its various parameters. Patch editing controls are divided into Pages. All of the controls for a given section are available at once in the multi-function Page Modifier section of the front panel.

All parameters of a sound are stored in memory, as well as a name for each sound program. Multi-Patches are used to program combinations of individual sounds. Since 12 voices (each may have a different sound) may be produced at once, a Multi-Patch saves the musician the nuisance of calling up each voice in the combination individually. Multi-Patches also memorize MIDI channel selection, panning, volume, transposition and detune data for each voice.

All in all the Matrix-12 offers an incredible amount of power and versatility, combining much of the best of both analog and digital synthesis. Perhaps Oberheim's claim that this is the ultimate analog synthesizer isn't just advertising hyperbole.

XPANDER SYNTHESIZER EXPANDER

Oberheim's Xpander, shown in Fig. 10-3, is a controllerless synthesizer intended to expand a multi-instrument MIDI system. Six voices can be controlled by external MIDI keyboards, sequencers or computers.

Each of the six voices is made up of the same elements as the voices in the Matrix-12. Voices and Multi-Patches are programmed in the same manner as on the Matrix-12 too. In fact, the Xpander is essentially a half-size Matrix-12 without the keyboard.

XK PROGRAMMABLE MIDI KEYBOARD CONTROLLER

Where the Xpander is a synthesizer without a controller, the Xk, shown in Fig. 10-4, is a controller without a synthesizer.

This five octave long-throw, touch-sensitive keyboard is used to control extra voices in a multi-instrument MIDI system.

The keyboard can be divided into three Zones, which may split the keyboard, or overlap for double or triple voicings. Each Zone may be assigned to any MIDI channel. Each Zone has a VOICE SPILLOVER feature. Extra notes are sent to the next MIDI channel.

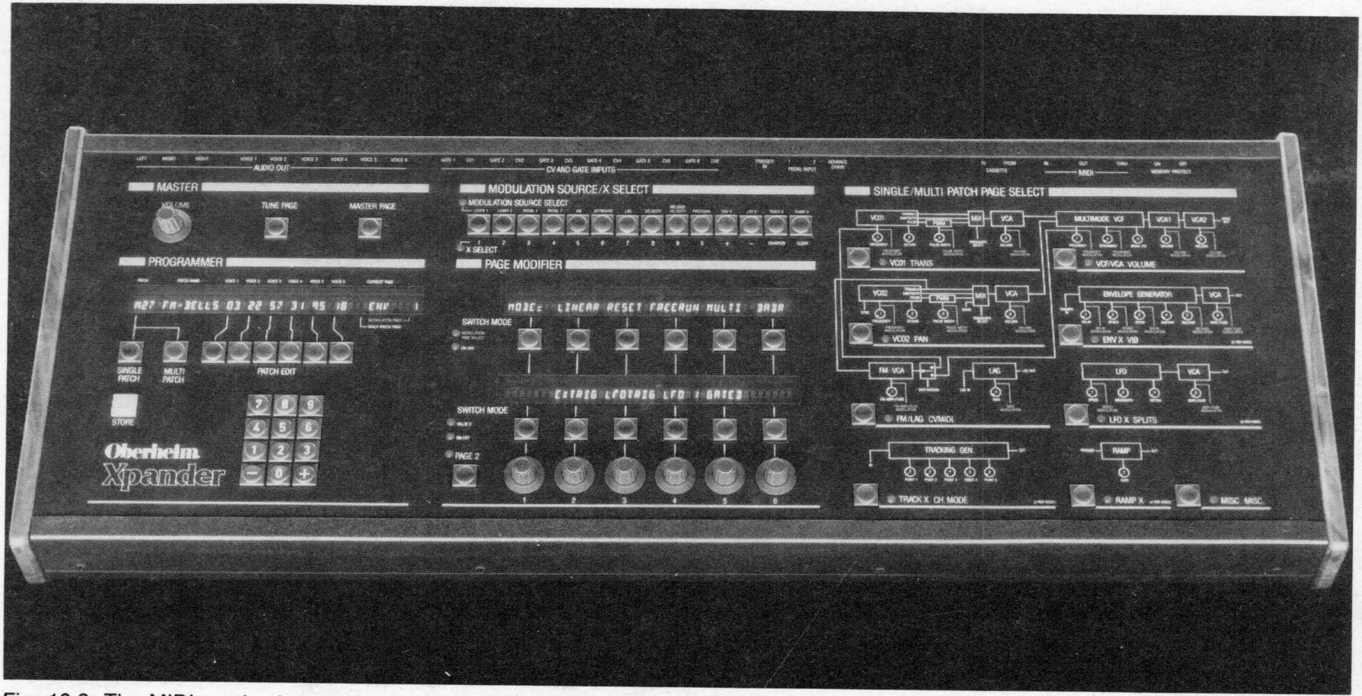

Fig. 10-3. The MIDI synthesis system can be expanded with the Oberheim Xpander.

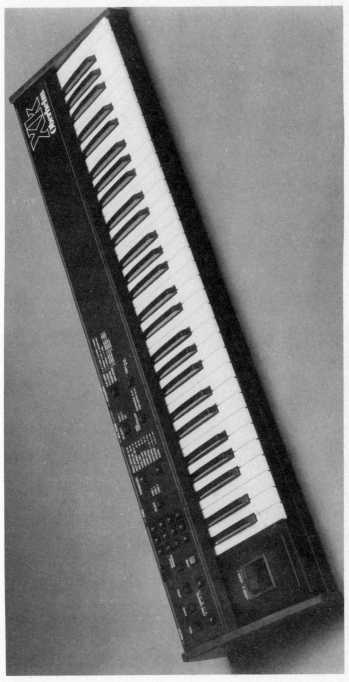

Fig. 10-4. The Xk is a remote keyboard for controlling MIDI instruments.

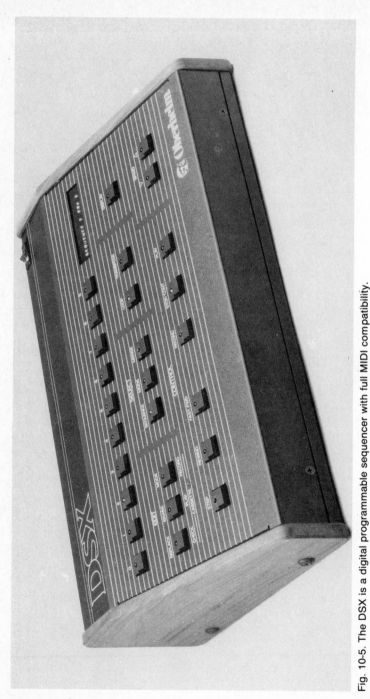

Fig. 10-5. The DSX is a digital programmable sequencer with full MIDI compatibility.

Zone settings can be stored in any of 99 Master Programs. Each program includes information on;

- MIDI channel for each Zone
- Patch number for each Zone
- size (number of notes) of each Zone
- MIDI Pressure
- Lever enable
- Mono mode enable
- transpositions

The Xk also features a sophisticated arpeggiator. Another useful feature is HOLD AND CHORD. A chord can be sustained then transposed with a single note.

DSX DIGITAL POLYPHONIC SEQUENCER

Oberheim also manufactures the DSX digital programmable sequencer, which is illustrated in Fig. 10-5. This unit is a far, far cry from the simple, repetitious analog sequencers of just a few years ago. This unit is essentially a computer dedicated to the composition, control, and manipulation of music.

The total memory capacity is 6000 notes. This can be divided into up to 10 sequences, each with 9 polyphonic Record Tracks with 16 note polyphony. These tracks can drive any MIDI equipped synthesizer.

Sequences can be combined into any of ten Merges. A Merge allows the DSX to perform any combination of sequences in any order or key. The tracks to be played for each Sequence may be selected.

Recorded sequences can be edited as needed. Pitch, tempo and timbre of each track may be independently altered. Individual tracks, sequences, and merges can be erased or copied. Full punch-in capabilities are supported to change even a single note.

An alpha-numeric display reads out programming and current status information.

The DSX also features "Quantization" to correct small errors in playing rhythms. High resolution Sync-to-Tape and Clock inputs and outputs are also provided.

11 | Korg/Unicord Synthesizers

Korg/Unicord (89 Frost St. Westbury, NY 11590) has been an important manufacturer of electronic musical instruments for a number of years now. As this chapter will demonstrate, they manufacture a wide range of products.

THE POLY-800 PROGRAMMABLE POLYPHONIC SYNTHESIZER

The POLY-800 is an eight voice digital synthesizer with a 64 program memory. It is MIDI equipped and has a full-size 4 octave keyboard.

A 256 note polyphonic sequencer is built into this instrument. Recorded sequences may be edited with relative ease.

Each voice is made up primarily of two DCOs (Digitally-Controlled Oscillators). Three DEGs (Digital Envelope Generators) are also provided. These DEGs produce six stage envelopes in a ADBSSR format;

- Attack
- Decay
- Break point
- Slope
- Sustain
- Release

This offers a lot more possibilities than the traditional ADSR format. Some typical ADBSSR envelopes are illustrated in Fig. 11-1.

The front panel of the POLY-800 is divided into 8 sections;

- VOLUME (also on/off)
- TUNE (slide control)
- JOYSTICK (for modulation effects and pitch bend)
- BEND (sets maximum pitch bend depth)
- SEQUENCER
- KEY ASSIGN MODES (discussed below)
- PROGRAMMER (discussed below)
- PARAMETER TABLE (discussed below)

In the KEY ASSIGN MODE section there are three buttons labelled A, B, and C. These correspond to the following keyboard modes;

- A POLY (8 and 4 voice polyphony)
- B CHORD MEMORY (play parallel harmonies using just one key—monophonic bass and solo articulation)
- C HOLD (sustained "hands off" sound)

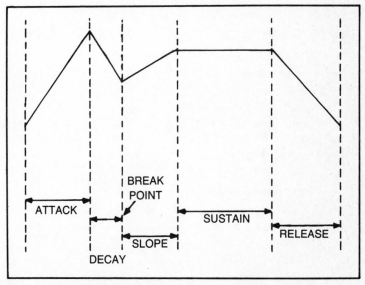

Fig. 11-1. The POLY-800 generates complex ADBSSR envelopes.

The PROGRAMMER section obviously is used to program the instrument. This section is made up of 8 controls;

- PROGRAM/PARA (switch between the program select and parameter select modes)
- SAVE (store voice or sequencer programs to cassette tape)
- LOAD (from cassette tape)
- VERIFY (check tape data against memory)
- CANCEL (stop current tape operation)
- WRITE (memorize a program)
- VALUE (display value of parameter selected via Up/Down buttons
- BANK HOLD (quick access to programs or parameters within the same bank

The PROGRAMMER section also features a large 6 digit LED readout to display data.

The PARAMETER TABLE section is a collection of displays to define all program parameters (waveform, cutoff frequency, envelope times, etc.). This section of the front panel is divided into 11 sub-sections corresponding to the "modules" making up the patch;

- DCO 1
  Octave
  Waveform
  16' to 2' harmonics
  level parameters
- MODE
  Whole (8 voices—one DCO per voice)
  Double (4 voices—two DCOs per voice)
- DCO 2
  (same as DCO1)
- NOISE
  (white noise generator with separate EG)
- VCF (24 dB/octave)
  cutoff frequency
  resonance
  keyboard tracking
  envelope polarity
  EG intensity
  multiple or single triggering

- CHORUS (stereo)
- DEG 1 (for DCO 1)
  - attack
  - decay
  - break point
  - slope
  - sustain
  - release
- DEG 2 (for DCO 2)
  - (same as DEG 1)
- DEG 3 (for VCF & Noise)
  - (same as DEG 1)
- MG (modulation)
  - frequency
  - delay
  - DCO
  - VCF
- MIDI
  - receive channel
  - program change
  - sequence clock

DW-6000 PROGRAMMABLE
DIGITAL WAVEFORM SYNTHESIZER

At the time of this writing, Korg's newest synthesizer was the DW-6000 Programmable Digital Waveform Synthesizer. The manufacturer claims that this is a digital device which actually responds like a musical instrument, allowing the musician numerous possibilities for expression.

Actually, the DW-6000 is a digital/analog hybrid, offering, to a large extent, the best of both worlds. It combines state-of-the-art Digital Waveform Generators (DWGs) and Digital Envelope Generators (DEGs) with analog Voltage-Controlled Filters (VCFs) and Voltage-Controlled Amplifiers (VCAs).

Each DWG can produce eight different waveforms, which are stored in a pair of 256K-bit ROM chips. The harmonic structures of these waveforms are richer and more complex than traditional electronic waveforms (rectangle waves, sawtooth waves, etc.). Korg claims the more complex harmonic textures provide greater realism to the synthesized sounds.

The DEGs are six stage (ADBSSR) envelope generators, and can create numerous unusual effects.

Analog VCFs and VCAs are employed in the DW-6000 for speedy access.

The full-size five octave keyboard is six voice polyphonic with portamento and stereo chorus effects. The keyboard may be programmed in POLY or UNISON modes.

This instrument is also programmable. Up to 64 sound programs may be stored for instant re-access. Programs can be sequentially switched via a foot-switch—a great convenience for live performances. The DW-6000 is fully MIDI compatible.

OTHER KORG INSTRUMENTS

Korg markets several other synthesizers, which we will mention, but not examine in depth.

The Korg POLY61M is a 6 voice polyphonic analog/digital hybrid. It is MIDI compatible and can store up to 64 voice programs.

The Korg POLYSIX appears to be a slightly stripped down version of the POLY61M. It has six voice polyphony, and can store up to 32 patch programs.

The Korg MONO/POLY is a fairly traditional analog synthesizer with monophonic (lead) and polyphonic modes. The MS-20 is an entirely monophonic version.

Korg also manufactures the EPS-1 electronic piano/string synthesizer, and two electronic organs (the CX-3 <portable> and the BX-3 <dual manual>).

The BPX-3 is a compact bass pedal system with harmonic synthesis for rich sound textures. A pedal keyboard (PK-13) is sold separately.

The EX-800 is a keyboardless programmable polyphonic synthesizer module for expanding MIDI based systems. It appears to be very similar to the POLY-800 discussed earlier.

A vaguely guitar shaped portable remote keyboard (RK-100) is also marketed by Korg. The RK-100 can be used to control any MIDI synthesizer. It is available in black, red, white, and walnut. Korg also makes several drum machines (discussed in Chapter 17) and accessories (discussed in Chapter 16).

12

Yamaha Synthesizers

Another popular synthesizer manufacturer is the Yamaha International Corporation (Professional Products Division, P.O. Box 6600, Buena Park, CA 90622).

DX7/DX9 DIGITAL SYNTHESIZERS

We will discuss the DX7 and DX9 digital synthesizers together because they are quite similar. The DX7 is shown in Fig. 12-1.

Both instruments are FM digital programmable algorithm synthesizers with 5 octave polyphonic keyboards.

Considerable programmability is offered on both models. Keyboard scaling of envelope rates and levels is programmable on both the DX7 and the DX9. The DX7 has slightly greater flexibility.

The front panels of these instruments are quite uncluttered, thanks to the digital technology. There are no knobs, just a few linear controls, and a number of buttons. Digital LED and LCD readouts are used to display data.

All of the synthesis modules (VCOs, VCFs, EGs, and VCAs) are digitally synthesized. The specific digital technique used in the DX series of synthesizers to create sounds is called FM (Frequency Modulation) Digital Synthesis, and the results can be quite impressive. Very realistic sounding effects can be achieved.

The DX7 comes supplied with 32 factory preset sounds, while the DX9 has 20 factory presets. Additional factory-supplied sound

Fig. 12-1. The DX7 is a popular MIDI synthesizer manufactured by Yamaha.

programs can be read from external storage media. The DX9 uses standard cassette tapes, while the DX7 uses plug-in EEPROM (Electrically Erasable Programmable Read Only Memory) cartridges.

In addition, the Dx7 has 26 programmable performance parameters. The DX9 has 20. Both instruments permit different timbre parameters. This data is stored in RAM (Random Access Memory). The RAM in both models is protected with battery backup to prevent loss of memory when the instrument is unplugged.

Voices are made up of "Operators." An operator is the digital combination of;

VCO (Voltage-Controlled Oscillator)
EG (Envelope Generator)
VCA (Voltage-Controlled Amplifier)

Each operator is essentially a digital sine wave generator. Operators are grouped into "algorithms." The overall output of each operator can be adjusted for Attack/Decay/Sustain/Release via the DX's unique envelope generator.

The DX7 has 6 operators that can be set up to form 32 different algorithms. The DX9 has just four operators which can be combined into 8 different algorithms.

Additional features of the DX7 and DX9 include;

- breath controller inputs
- jack for portamento foot pedal
- jack for sustain foot pedal
- jack for volume foot pedal
- jack for modulation foot pedal (DX7 only)
- programmable modulation wheel
- MIDI interface (DX7 only)

The DX7 also features a pitch envelope generator. This allows you to program automatic pitch bending in the ADSR (Attack—Decay—Sustain—Release) format. The pitch envelope generator is not included in the DX9. The suggested retail price is $2000 for the DX7 and $1400 for the simpler DX9.

DX1 PROGRAMMABLE FM DIGITAL SYNTHESIZER

The technology of the DX7 and DX9 is carried even further in the deluxe DX1, shown in Fig. 12-2.

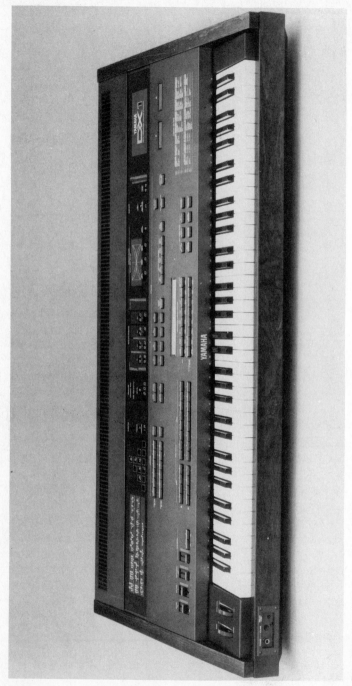

Fig. 12-2. The DX1 is an advanced, expanded version of the DX7.

The 73 note keyboard on this powerful instrument has full-sized wooden keys, and a precision, weighted return action. The return action gives the keyboard a very natural feel, similar to that of an acoustic piano.

As in the DX7 and DX9, the modules in the DX1 are digitally synthesized. This instrument has two voice generation channels, each with 6 operators (per voice) and 32 algorithms (memorized voices). In other words, up to 64 different voices can be stored in the DX1's memory.

The two voice channels can be operated in three different modes;

- single
- dual
- split

In the single mode, only one voice channel is active, of course. Either channel A or channel B may be selected. This mode features 64 memory positions. Up to 32 notes may be simultaneously sounded.

Both channels are utilized in the dual mode. The output in this mode is stereophonic. Up to 16 notes may be simultaneously sounded.

In the split mode, the keyboard can be divided at any point. The channel A voice is played on the upper portion of the keyboard, and the channel B voice is played on the lower portion. Each channel is 16 note polyphonic.

The display system on the DX1 is very sophisticated and useful. Each control tab has an independent LED on/off indicator. In addition, the status of all programming information to be edited is shown on an extensive LED display panel. The parameters and data being modified flash in the Edit mode. Bar graphs are shown on the display to indicate the status of many functions, including;

- algorithms
- detune
- envelope generator
- frequency ratios
- output level
- velocity sensitivity

The control panel of the DX1 also includes a forty character alphanumeric LCD panel. This panel is back-lit to maximize readability. This display reads out different types of information when the synthesizer is in different modes. Some of the data displayed on the LCD panel includes;

- control prompts
- function name & data
- memory position
- performance memory name
- voice name

The control panel of the DX1 is fairly simple, considering the complexity of the instrument. Most of the switches have multiple functions that are selected by the number of times they are pressed. A silk screen "job table" for function location is provided to help the user keep track of what's going on.

In addition to the multi-function switches, the control panel of the DX1 has only six controls—four slide pots, and two wheels. The slider functions are;

- balance between channels A & B
- data entry
- portamento time
- volume

The wheels control;

- modulation depth
- pitch bend

These functions are completely programmable. This instrument is fully MIDI compatible, and retails for just under $11,000.

CX5M MUSIC COMPUTER

Figure 12-3 shows Yamaha's CX5M Music Computer. This is a full-fledged Z80 based microcomputer with Microsoft's MSX BASIC built in. (MSX is a trademark of Microsoft, Inc.) A number of MSX program cartridges are available, including games, word processing, and business applications. The system also features high resolution 16 color graphics. But our main interest here is that the CX5M was designed specifically with musical applications in mind.

Fig. 12-3. The CX5M Music Computer is a full-fledged microcomputer system designed specifically for musical applications.

111

The CX5M has a built-in FM Sound Synthesizer, similar to those used in the DX1, DX7, and DX9. Since the CX5M is also MIDI compatible, it can be readily combined with these (and other) instruments.

There are 46 pre-programmed voices that can be easily accessed with built-in software. Voices can be recorded and immediately played back. Up to 2000 notes can be stored. An auto-accompaniment section, featuring bass, chords, and rhythm, is also provided.

Optional keyboards may be added to the system to create a real-time synthesizer package, as illustrated in Fig. 12-4. Two compatible keyboards are marketed by Yamaha. The YK-01 has small keys, and retails for $100. Full sized keys are provided on the YK-10, which currently sells for $200.

Anything played on the keyboard can be recorded into the computer's memory, and played back exactly as it was originally played.

Yamaha also sells several plug-in cartridge software packages for the CX5M. Each software package retails for $50.

YRM101 FM Music Composer

As the name suggests, this program is a composition/orchestration aid. A musical staff is displayed on the computer's screen, and notes can be entered either from the computer's alphanumeric keyboard, or the optional music keyboard. With the optional music keyboard, music can be scored as you play it, which can be extremely handy.

The system supports up to eight separate parts. Each part can be assigned an "instrument" (one of the preprogrammed voices, or a user programmed voice). The music can be played directly from the score. The score can also be used as a super-sequencer for MIDI compatible devices, such as synthesizers and drum machines.

You're not limited to just indicating the notes themselves. This software package also provides full control over such musical features as;

- dynamics
- key signature
- phrasing
- tempo
- time signature

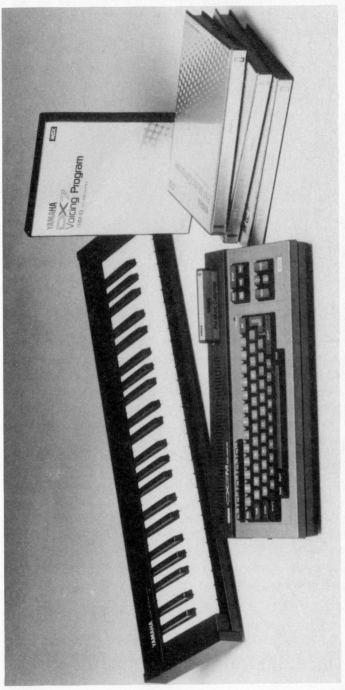

Fig. 12-4. Optional keyboards may be added to the CX5M to create a real time synthesis package.

Many common musical effects may also be notated. These include standard markings for;

- accelerando
- accents
- atempo
- crescendo
- decrescendo
- fermata
- legato
- ritardando
- sforzando
- staccato

Compositions can be stored on standard cassette tape, and reloaded whenever desired.

YRM102 FM Voicing Program

This software package is a powerful tool for creating and modifying voices produced by the the FM Voice Generator. Full control is given over all parameters. Voices can be edited as desired.

The system employs four operators and a choice of 8 algorithms (see the description of the DX7/9). Each operator has its own envelope generator for a tremendous variety of possible effects.

YRM103 DX7 Voicing Program

This software package allows you to use the CX5M to add significantly to the programmability of the DX7. The synthesizer and the computer are connected via their MIDI interfaces.

The primary advantage here is that the voice parameter data is presented in graphic form, which is a lot easier to understand and use than a bunch of abstract numbers.

YRM104 FM Music Macro

This software package allows you to employ the system's music capabilities in your own BASIC programs.

Other music software packages will undoubtably be added to the line in the near future. The current list price for the CX5M Music Computer is $470.

Fig. 12-5. The TX816 system is made up of 8 TF1 FM Tone Generation Modules.

MIDI FM TONE GENERATION SYSTEMS

The Yamaha TF1 tone module is a MIDI compatible synthesizer expansion module. It is essentially a DX7 synthesizer without a keyboard. It can store up to 32 voices with function data including pitch end, portamento, and modulation wheel settings for each voice. A TF1 tone module retails for $545.

The TX216 is a pair of TF1s in a 19 inch rack mountable frame. It sells for $2100.

An even larger system is the TX816, shown in Fig. 12-5. It includes 8 TF1s in a 19 inch rack mountable frame. The current price for the TX816 system is $5000.

QX1 DIGITAL MIDI SEQUENCE RECORDER

Yamaha also makes a computer controlled, MIDI compatible sequencer, called the QX1. It digitally records real time performances from a MIDI keyboard. Up to eight tracks of music can be recorded. Track bouncing is possible, and since it is recorded in the form of digital data, there is no signal degradation.

The QX1 also features full editing capabilities. A musical piece can be composed step by step rather than real time if you prefer. Each individual note can be modified any way you like.

A data sequence/composition can be stored on a computer floppy disk. A single standard 5¼" floppy disk can store more than 80,000 notes, which is about as much music as is recorded on a standard LP album.

13

Sequential Circuits

Sequential Circuits, Inc. (3051 North First St. San Jose, CA 95134) strongly established themselves as a leader in the electronic music world with their popular Prophet synthesizer. There have been several versions of this instrument over the years.

THE PROPHET T8

The current Prophet synthesizer is called the Prophet T8. The "T" refers to the touch-sensitive keyboard, while the "8" represents the eight voice capability of this synthesizer. The Prophet T8 is a programmable type instrument.

The touch sensitive keyboard covers 6 ½ octaves (76 keys). The key action is designed to give the feel of an acoustic piano keyboard. Both velocity and pressure sensitivity are provided. Key to key consistency is quite exact. A highly reliable optical system is used to determine the key velocity two ways—as the key is depressed, and as it is released. The velocity data is transmitted to the envelope generators to interact with the Attack/Decay and Release controls. The pressure sensor is independent for each individual key. It can control any or all of the following seven parameters;

- AMP (volume)
- FILTER
- FREQ A (sharp pitch)

- FREQ B (flat pitch)
- LFO AMOUNT
- LFO FREQ
- PW (pulse width)

When multiple keys are depressed, the resulting modulation is independently articulated. On many other pressure sensitive synthesizers it is monophonically averaged, or controlled by the key that is pressed the hardest. The musician playing the Prophet T8 has quite a bit of expressive control at his fingertips.

The keyboard may be played in any of four modes;

- SINGLE
- DOUBLE
- UNISON
- SPLIT

In the SINGLE mode, a single voice is played across the entire keyboard. In the DOUBLE mode, two sounds are triggered by each key across the entire keyboard. All eight voices are activated by a single key in the UNISON mode, allowing for very thick choral textures. The SPLIT mode, of course, splits the keyboard, with one voice being controlled by the lower portion of the keyboard and a second voice being controlled by the upper portion of the keyboard and a second voice being controlled by the upper portion of the keyboard. The split point is programmable.

Each voice consists of;

- 2 VCOs
- 1 VCF
- 1 noise source
- 2 ADSR envelope generators
- 1 low-pass VCF

Each of the two VCOs can produce ascending sawtooth, triangle, or rectangle waves. The pulse width of the rectangle waves is adjustable. The two oscillators may be synchronized together if desired, or they may be left in a free-running mode. The second VCO may be controlled by the LFO or the keyboard. The VCF features an adjustable tracking control.

Extensive modulation control is provided. This is called POLY-MODULATION on the control panel. POLY-MODULATION interacts with the velocity sensing keyboard. It can also invert waveform envelopes to widen the range of available sounds.

The Prophet T8 is fully programmable. It comes with 128 pre-programmed patches (voices). The user can also program his own sounds. The Prophet T8 is MIDI compatible.

SIX-TRACK

Another offering from Sequential Circuits is the Six-Track programmable, Multi-timbral synthesizer. Up to six completely different sounds may be played at once. All voices may be played live on the keyboard, or they may be recorded one track at a time on the built-in six track sequencer/recorder, which can store more than 700 notes.

This instrument is fully programmable. Each voice is made up of the following modules;

- 1 multi-waveform analog VCO
- 1 resonant 4-pole low-pass VCF
- 1 VCA
- 3 ADSR envelope generators
- 1 LFO

There are 100 sounds pre-programmed in the Six-Track's memory. The user can program additional voices of his own.

The Six-Track also includes the following special features;

- arpeggiator
- filter FM
- inverted envelope options
- modulation wheel
- pitch-bend wheel
- polyglide

The arpeggiator functions in two modes. A chord may be arpeggiated in the traditional up/down manner, or in the order the keys were depressed.

Two unison modes are featured on this instrument. One is the standard UNISON in which all six voices play a single sound polyphonically. The other mode is called STACK. Up to six different monophonic sounds can be layered for unique voicings.

A LEGATO switch is included to control the keyboard triggering mode. With LEGATO on, the envelope generators will be retriggered when all keys are released. All of the notes will articulate under the same envelope. When LEGATO is turned off, of course, the keyboard triggers an envelope for each key as it is depressed in the usual manner.

This instrument is MIDI compatible. A Model 64 Sequencer is available to interface the Six-Track directly with a Commodore 64 computer. The computer is used as a powerful digital recorder with up to 4000 notes of memory and powerful editing features.

MAX

The Max is advertised as a multi-timbred polyphonic keyboard which allows up to six completely different sounds to be simultaneously played. This can be done live, directly from the keyboard, or built up a track at a time on the built-in digital sequencer/recorder. Like the Six-Track, the Max's sequencer has six track capability. In fact, this instrument appears to be essentially a somewhat stripped down version of the Six-Track. Like Sequential Circuits' other synthesizers, the Max is MIDI compatible.

14
The Synclavier

The Synclavier by New England Digital Corp. (49 N. Main St., Box 546, White River Junction, VT 05001) is the Rolls Royce of sound synthesis systems—almost everybody's dream system and priced to match. It's power and versatility make it worth the hefty price tag, but it is far beyond the budget of the majority of musicians. A basic "starter" system costs $21,500. Various options can double the price.

There might be a tendency to just say, "Well, I'll never afford that!" and move on to the next chapter. Even if you don't have that kind of money, it will be worth your while to gain some familiarity with this deluxe instrument. It is almost an ideal standard that other, lower priced instruments try to shoot for. Since this device offers almost all features found on modern digital synthesizers, studying the Synclavier gives you a convenient way to compare the various features, and decide which are most important to you.

The control panel is about as simple as it can get. It consists of:

- Two line (32 character) alphanumeric LED display
- 160 lighted push-buttons (divided into 6 convenient sections)
- A single multi-purpose tuning knob

The instrument can automatically tune itself to A—440 Hz (concert standard).

Over 320 pre-programmed voices are provided. The musician can program millions of other voices.

In its most basic form, the Synclavier has 8 voices. It is also available in 16, 24, and 32 voice versions. You can even special order a 128 voice model. The keyboard covers a full six and a half octaves.

Looking at the Synclavier's control panel from left to right we find;

- The Master Control Knob (used to make changes on all parameters)
- 32 character Readout
- Timbre Parameters section (digital oscillator and envelopes)
- 32 Track Digital Memory Recorder
- Timbre/Sequence Storage section (for storing and recalling sounds and compositions)
- Keyboard Control section
- Timbre Control section (vibrato/stereo/portamento)
- Real-Time Effects section

While fully computerized, the user doesn't need to learn programming. Everything is accomplished with clearly labeled multiple select buttons and the master control knob. It might take you a little while to learn how to make a maximum use of the Synclavier's capabilities, but you can get started very quickly, regardless of previous experience (or lack of experience).

The Synclavier's memory system is essentially a 32 track digital recorder. New England Digital claims it is even more powerful than a professional 4 track tape recorder. All notes and effects are recorded directly from the six and a half octave keyboard.

Up to 32 completely independent parts (in completely different voices) can be recorded, and played back in perfect sync in any combination. Up to 32 voices can even be recorded on a single track (although they can't be separated for playback).

The digital recorder certainly isn't limited to just simple recording and playback. Additional functions include;

- automatic rhythm correction (the click track can be subdivided by any number between 1 and 32 to enable very precise rhythms)
- fast forward

- insert, chain, and delete to serve the functions of a digital drum machine
- reverse
- separate outputs for each of the 32 tracks are possible (up to 64 total)
- slide recorded tracks backwards or forwards in time instantly
- variable pitch (without altering speed)
- variable speed (without altering pitch)

Other functions of the Synclavier include:

- 192 different patching capabilities
- continue button to resume performance of interrupted recordings
- digital metronome
- double command erase button to prevent accidental erasures
- "Help" button
- 76 note keyboard
- keyboard transposition
- keyboard control over volume envelope, FM plus dynamic envelopes
- keyboard is velocity and pressure (after-touch) sensitive (programmable)
- loop button to repeat any set of recorded notes automatically. Up to 32 independent loops can be set up
- pressure control over:
      Repeat/Arpeggiate
      Stereo effects
      Vibrato
- programmable names for stored timbres (voices)
- programmable modulation wheel
- programmable pitch bend
- all real-time effects are memorized for later editing and playback
- ribbon controller (programmable)
- SKT (Select Keyboard Timbre)—any part of a previously recorded voice on a track can be altered without re-recording
- SMT (Select Memory Timbre)—the voice recorded on any track can be instantly replaced, without changing the notes.
- solo any track, or combine any combination of tracks for playback

- track bouncing and mix-down techniques are possible, similar to a multi-track analog tape recorder
- two special sync modes to synchronize the Synclavier with any multi-track tape machine, drum machine, or other external equipment

The loop function is similar to a standard sequencer, but it has several significant advantages. The starting point and number of notes in the loop can be determined by the user. The loop does not have to return to the first note of memory. Up to 32 independent loops may be defined. In addition, an unlimited number of internal loops is possible.

On-Line Information Available

The synthesis method used in the Synclavier is rather unique. New England Digital calls this method "partial timbres." Each partial timbre is made up of 36 or more separately adjustable harmonics. An 8 voice Synclavier system has capabilities for up to 8 partial timbres (or channels of sound). The 16 voice system has 16 partial timbres, the 24 voice system has 24, and so forth.

Up to four independent partial timbres can be simultaneously keyed from the keyboard. This means you can make up a rich, complex voice with up to 134 harmonic components! The large number of available harmonics allows for fuller, more natural sounding voices than are available from most synthesizers.

The chorus function carries you even further. Up to sixteen partial timbres can be active on each key, for a remarkable total of up to 384 harmonic components.

The chorus effect may be used on all or individual partial timbres. This effect can enhance the sound of partial timbres and mix them with the originals for rich, orchestral effects. Echo effects are also possible with the chorus function.

The Synclavier can also employ sampling techniques. An acoustic sound can be recorded, and later resynthesized. Of course the recorded sound can be manipulated many different ways before it is reproduced. The software in the Synclavier builds up a partial timbre from a series of "timbre frames." During the note, these timbre frames are spliced together in smooth, easily controlled crossfade. These time varying aspects of the note produce a more natural sound.

The tremendous amount of harmonic control is exciting in itself, but the Synclavier offers even greater control of each sound. Most analog synthesizers offered only 2, 3, or 4 stage envelopes (Attack/Release—Attack/Sustain/Release—Attack/Decay/Sustain /Release). The synclavier features six stage envelopes:

Delay
Attack
Peak
Initial Decay
Sustain
Final Decay

Some typical envelopes that can be generated by this system are illustrated in Fig. 14-1. The initial decay can be reversed to serve as a secondary attack, as shown in Fig. 14-2.

Independent six stage envelope generators are provided for amplitude (volume) and harmonic envelopes. The timbre can change with time. The effect is similar to driving an analog VCF with an envelope generator.

Even more versatility is offered with a separate keyboard decay adjust for envelopes. Separate keyboard control of stereo placement or effects is also provided.

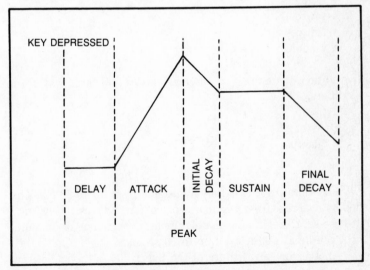

Fig. 14-1. The Synclavier produces six stage envelopes.

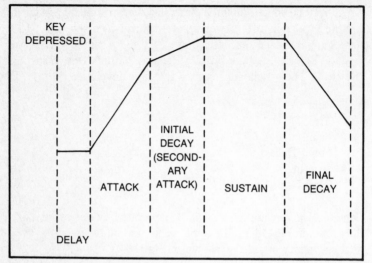

Fig. 14-2. The initial decay can be reversed to serve as a secondary attack.

Vibrato effects are completely adjustable on the Synclavier. Four independent vibrato generators are provided, each with five basic waveforms:

- sine
- triangle
- sawtooth
- square
- random

In addition, there are two patching modes and three waveform modifiers;

- invert
- quantize
- raise

The vibrato speed is fully adjustable from 0.1 to 50 Hz. The depth range runs from zero to a sweep of four octaves. The vibrato may be set to begin immediately upon the beginning of the note, or it can be attack delayed up to 10 seconds.

Another unusual feature of the Synclavier is the completely polyphonic portamento. Complete chords can slide together on the keyboard. Alternatively, up to four different portamento rates can be set up on the keyboard at the same time. Each portamento rate can be adjusted from 0 to 50 seconds. The independent portamento can even slide in different directions at once (one going up the scale, while a second is going down the scale).

The Synclavier also features a completely controllable decay adjust. On some acoustic instruments, such as the piano, lower notes tend to have a longer decay than higher notes. This control allows the musician to simulate this effect.

Automatic arpeggiate is another feature of the Synclavier. When a chord is played on the keyboard, the individual notes of the chord will be sounded repeatedly in sequence, at a rate which is adjustable from 0 to 100 Hz. This function would be used to simulate guitar or mandolin strums, instrumental trills, xylophone rolls, and other such effects.

Closely related to the Automatic Arpeggiate is the Automatic Repeat. As long as a key (or keys) are held down, the note (or chord) will be repeatedly sounded at a rate adjustable from 0 to 100 Hz.

Memorized data (voices, note sequences, effects, multi-part compositions, or whatever) can be stored indefinitely on floppy disks. A single disk can hold a great deal of information that can be individually retrieved in seconds. Changing disks is a simple 10 second task, so it is very easy to build up an unlimited library. The floppy disk system is also used to allow the user to conveniently install software updates from the factory.

The Synclavier can be used with a modem to communicate with another instrument anywhere in the world over the standard telephone lines.

The power of this system can be increased by accessing the internal microcomputer with the Terminal Support Option. Three programs are available for use with the Synclavier and a terminal. Each is fully compatible with the Synclavier's real-time keyboard. These programs are:

GRAPHICS—a real-time display of timbral information
MAX—a software programming language
SCRIPT—a "score processor"—similar to a word processor, but for music

Clearly the Synclavier offers a lot of power for its high price. Whether or not that much power is worth the investment is a decision that can only be made by the individual musician, and the intended application.

Kawai

Kawai Musical Instrument Mfg., Co., Ltd. of Japan makes a number of fine electronic musical instruments.

ELECTRIC PIANOS

This firm manufactures a line of high quality electric pianos. Unlike many electronic pianos, these instruments start out with the same acoustic sound mechanism used in traditional non-electric pianos. Hammers strike steel strings as the keys are depressed. This gives the musician the full range of dynamic control the piano is noted for. Obviously, the feel of the keyboard is the same as for a true piano action.

The sound is electronically picked up, and amplified, with or without modification.

Three basic "voices" are made available, via three push buttons on the control panel:

- PIANO 1 — acoustic
- PIANO 2 — hard
- PIANO 3 — brilliant

These "voices" may be used in any combination, giving the musician the choice of seven basic sounds.

A CHORUS effect is also provided, for even greater variety of sound.

Kawai's electric pianos come in three models. The standard model is the EP-705. The EP-608 is a compact portable instrument. The EP-308 is an electric grand piano.

THE SX-240
PROGRAMMABLE POLYPHONIC SYNTHESIZER

Kawai also manufacturers a powerful eight voice polyphonic synthesizer, called the SX-240. This unit is fully programmable for 40 sound sound parameters. A built-in cassette interface is included to allow long term storage of programs.

Two separate voices can be layered together when the keyboard is put into its DUAL mode. A SPLIT mode can also be used to control two different voices from different portions of the keyboard. The 37 highest keys control one voice, while the 24 lower keys operate the second voice. Three different SPLIT combinations are offered for dividing the eight available voices between the sections of the keyboard:

- 6 lower/2 upper
- 4 lower/4 upper
- 2 lower/6 upper

This synthesizer also features a built-in real-time polyphonic sequencer. Up to 1500 notes can be digitally stored for later playback. Eight independent sequences of approximately 200 notes each may be recorded. For longer sequences, these 200 note "modules" may be chained together.

An alphanumeric LED display is included on the control panel. Patches can be assigned actual names, like FLUTE, or TRUMPET. This way you don't have to remember that patch program #12 produces a flute sound, and patch #9 is a trumpet sound. The SX-240 is MIDI compatible.

16
Wersi Organs

As electronic music technology has evolved, many synthesis techniques have been applied to electronic organs. The distinction between organs and synthesizers has been blurring. In this chapter we will examine some high technology electronic organs from Wersi USA (1720 Hempstead Rd. P.O. Box 5318, Lancaster, PA 17601). This company specializes in console organ kits. Many of their recent products have crossed over the line, and might be considered synthesizers.

ALPHA DX300

One of Wersi's most popular instruments is the Alpha DX300. The company says it is comparable to instruments in the $10,000 to $20,000 price range, but the assembled version retails for only about $7500. Like most Wersi products, the Alpha DX300 is also available in kit form. The basic organ kit sells for just $2450.

Wersi prides themselves on the simplicity of their kits, and the thoroughness of their manuals. They claim that even someone with no prior experience in electronic construction can build the Alpha DX300 in under a week. I'd strongly recommend starting out with a few simpler, low-cost kits, before tackling a project of this size. If nothing else, the novice needs some practice in making good solder joints. Your first project should be low enough in cost that it won't be a disaster if you accidentally damage it.

Even so, Wersi kits are designed with the amateur strongly in mind. If you can read, you should be able to follow their construction manuals without undue difficulty.

The Alpha DX300 is a digital, computer based instrument, and its sound generation modules are in software form. Therefore, the assembled and kit versions will result in identical sounds. No complicated calibration procedures are required.

This instrument is MIDI compatible and is designed to be interfaced with a personal computer. The computer can control the organ, or it can be used to display and analyze the notes being played on the keyboard.

Being so strongly software based, the Alpha DX300 is essentially obsolescence-proof. No additional equipment is needed to upgrade the system—just a new program tape, which can cost as little as $9. That is a pretty inexpensive upgrade.

Some of the programmable "accessories" for the Alpha DX300 include;

- Digital Drums
- Digital Reverb
- Drawbar sounds (like the old B3)
- Microphone Mixer
- Polyphonic Digital Synthesizer
- Sequencer/ Auto-accompaniment
- String Synthesis

The Alpha DX300 is a very compact and portable instrument. It weighs only 65 pounds, and includes its own amplifier and two monitor speakers.

Even though the Alpha DX300 is designed to be interfaced with a computer and/or load programs from a cassette, these items aren't necessary to make music with the instrument. It can be played directly like an ordinary organ without any external software.

The following functions are standard in the Alpha DX300;

- 39 preset solo voices, including:
  — brass
  — liturgical organ
  — pan-flute (with air sound)
  — theater organ
  — tuba
  — vocal chorus
  — zither

131

- Piano/ Harpsichord (on both manuals)
- Concert/ Rock Guitar (with all the characteristics of its acoustic counterpart)
- String Orchestra (chamber orchestra or 100 violins)
- Synthesound and Phaser cannon (Star Wars)—wild electronic sounds
- Full set of professional drawbars
- Realistic live recorded drums
- Auto-accompaniment with any of the organ's voices
- Transposition to any key in half-tone steps

All of these sounds are fully polyphonic and are pre-programmed in the basic organ kit.

The same drawbar set is used for the upper and lower manuals and the pedal board. They are fully programmable, so complex changes can be made very quickly and easily.

In many respects, the Alpha DX300 is an advanced electronic organ with a full-featured synthesizer built-in. Some might consider it "the best of both worlds."

OTHER WERSI INSTRUMENTS

Wersi also makes a number of other organ kits, including the Beta DX400, the Delta DX500, and the Gamma DX500. These instruments use the same basic technology as the Alpha DX300, with a number of additional features.

The Condor DX100 is a digital multi-sound synthesizer. It looks much like a combo organ, and is ideal for stage work.

Wersi also makes electric pianos. The Pianostar T is a portable stage model. For a more permanent location, you might prefer the Grand piano, with its pressure-sensitive seven octave keyboard.

Accessories

As versatile as synthesizers are, it seems they can never do quite enough of what you want them to do. So along come the "add-ons" to be interfaced with your synthesizer, when possible. If system expansion seems at all possible for your needs in the future, it would probably be a good idea for you to choose a unit that can be readily interfaced to additional equipment.

J.L. COOPER MIDI ACCESSORIES

J.L. Cooper Electronics (1931 Pontius Ave., West Los Angeles, CA 90025) manufactures several powerful and practical add-on devices for MIDI systems. Some examples are shown in Fig. 17-1. Many of these devices help simplify large MIDI systems, or allow non-MIDI equipment to be used with MIDI instruments.

MIDI Switch Boxes

If you have more than two or three MIDI devices, the odds are strong that you will frequently need to change the arrangement of the system. This involves plugging and unplugging the various connecting cables. This is not only a major nuisance, it can add considerable wear and tear to the cables and connectors.

A switch box solves these types of problems very neatly. The various MIDI devices are connected to the switch box. The positions of the switches define the routing of the signals. This

Fig. 17-1. J.L. Cooper Electronics makes several MIDI accessories.

serves the same purpose as physically rearranging the cables, without all the hassles. J.L. Cooper makes several MIDI switch boxes.

Their MSB-1 accepts up to eight source inputs, and routes them to up to ten destination outputs. This compact unit is designed for convenient rack mounting. It's price is currently just under $400.

The MSB-2 is a more advanced model, with an internal microprocessor for control of the MIDI signals. This switch box can be remotely controlled. Numerical LED displays are used to indicate the current switching configuration.

Up to 16 different "patch" configurations can be stored in an internal memory, any of which can be selected with a single button. A MIDI program change command can also call up one of the previously stored "patches". This memory is battery backed-up.

The MSB-2 accepts up to eight source inputs, and can route them to up to sixteen destination outputs. The current price for this unit is just under $1200, factory direct.

Cooper also offers a third MIDI switch box (MSB-3). This unit is the simplest of the three, and retails for $220. It accepts up to two MIDI inputs, and routes them to up to four MIDI outputs. Signal routing can be controlled via a foot switch. Two "programmed patches" can be set up with manual switches. The two programs can be toggled back and forth with the foot switch (which is also hand operable). An LED display indicates which of the "programs" is currently in effect.

Finally, the MSB-4 is Cooper's simplest MIDI switch box. It is used to select whether or not a single MIDI slave device is connected or not to its master device. An LED indicates when the MIDI device is activated. The power source (a 9 volt battery, or optional 9 volt wall transformer) is only used for the LED indicator. MIDI operation is not affected by a dead battery. This unit is currently priced at $75.

MIDI Channelizer

Cooper's MIDI Channelizer is another handy device for solving problems that can crop up in complex MIDI systems. Problems can arise when the musician tries to connect almost all currently available MIDI synthesizers to some multi-channel MIDI sequencers. Many multi-channel MIDI sequencers expect the synthesizer to indicate the appropriate channel number for each note. For example, if you want to play a sequence of notes through channel 2, the synthesizer must send channel 2 indicators with the notes. However, most current MIDI synthesizers are designed so that they can't send any channel other than channel 1, even if they can be switched to other channels for playback. As a result, the musician can't call up more than a single voice at a time.

The MIDI channelizer allows the user to set any channel number on notes passing through it. This allows the musician to tap the full power of the sequencer(s) in his system.

MIDI Channel Filter

Another multi-channel sequencer problem is that many currently available MIDI synthesizers are capable of receiving only OMNI ON mode notes. In the OMNI ON mode, the synthesizer ignores channel numbers, and just plays all notes it receives. Once again, this gets in the way of taking full advantage of the capabilities of multi-channel MIDI sequencers. Cooper's MIDI Channel Filter allows the user to define which channel that the attached synthesizer will operate on. Even MIDI synthesizers with no multi-channel capabilities at all may be used. The Cooper MIDI Channel Filter is currently priced at $235.

MIDI Sync Devices

One of the big advantages of the MIDI system is the capability of synchronizing various instruments with each other. Unfortunately, many current devices can't directly realize the full sync capabilities implied by the MIDI approach. This is especially true when you want to interface older equipment with newer MIDI devices.

The MicroSync is a low cost ($175) device for syncing drum machines and sequencers that require different clock rates. Clock rates of 24, 48, and 96 pulses per quarter note are available.

The MIDI Drum Slave is used to control MIDI drum boxes via a drum pad set, or by pickups installed inside traditional drums. The "straight" sound can thereby be electronically or digitally enhanced. The MIDI signals can also be recorded into a sequencer, as if the drummer was playing a synthesizer.

This unit has 12 drum input channels, each with its own internal sensitivity control. The Hi-Hat open/close option is switch selectable.

The MIDI Brain Driver converts input MIDI notes into pulses simulating the signals from an electronic drumpad kit. Electronic drum kits can therefore be played by any MIDI controller, such as a synthesizer, a computer, or a sequencer. Both the MIDI Drum Slave and the MIDI Brain Driver are now priced at $650 each.

MIDI Interfacing Devices

Before the MIDI standards were developed, it was every synthesizer make for themselves. Synthesis equipment was designed to be self-contained. If any outboard accessories were available, they were brand specific. A Moog sequencer, for example, couldn't be directly connected to an Oberheim synthesizer. MIDI changed all that. Modern digital MIDI equipment can be interfaced in many ways, greatly increasing the power and versatility of your instruments.

There's still a lot of perfectly good older analog equipment out there. Electronic instruments have never been cheap, and very few musicians can afford to just shrug and say, "Well, that synthesizer is obsolete now, so I won't use it anymore." In an ideal world, there'd be some way to connect these older existing analog instruments to the newer, state-of-the-art digital MIDI devices.

Unfortunately, it's not quite an ideal world. But J.L. Cooper Electronics manufactures several interfacing devices to achieve a fairly good compromise.

The MIDI Interface 1out accepts digital MIDI input information and outputs analog control voltages, and gating signals, which can be used with most older synthesis equipment. This device conforms to the old pseudo-standard (it wasn't adhered to by all manufacturers) of 1 Volt/Octave.

Some analog synthesizers require positive gating pulses (such as Moog), while others call for negative gating pulses (such as Arp and Oberheim). The MIDI Interface 1out can accommodate both.

This unit has eight main CV/Gate channels. Internal circuitry senses which channels are in use, and routes incoming MIDI notes to the appropriate active channels. A ninth CV channel is also available for use in Pitch Bend and similar modulation effects.

For just $750, it is possible to update "old-fashioned" analog synthesis equipment for use in a modern MIDI system.

A simpler, stripped down version (the MIDI CV 1N) is also available for just under $300.

The MIDI Interface 1in works on the same basic principles, but in the opposite direction. It converts control voltage and gating signals from an analog synthesizer or sequencer into appropriate MIDI data. This unit is currently priced at $650.

A simpler, stripped down version (the MIDI CV 1N) is also available for approximately $275.

J.L. Cooper also markets some MIDI interfacing devices for specific analog instruments. For example, a MIDI Interface Kit can be installed in the Oberheim OB-Xa synthesizer. The MIDI OberFace allows the popular Oberheim DSX sequencer to be employed as a stand-alone MIDI sequencer. The MIDI Chromaface adds MIDI capabilities to the Rhodes CHROMA.

MIDI Lighting Controller

The MIDI system is designed to transmit data for sound synthesis functions to be passed among various pieces of digital equipment. But a digital control code is a digital control code. MIDI does not have to be used just for sound synthesis. The MLC-1 is a MIDI lighting controller. It provides a convenient method of synchronizing light shows to the music. Lighting changes could also be controlled by a MIDI sequencer, or a computer.

This unit, which can accurately synchronize to within a sixteenth note, normally can control up to 12 lighting channels. As an option this can be expanded to 24.

The MLC-1 also has four (eight in the expanded version) on/off outputs. These can be used to synchronize special effects such as flash pots.

Song Store II

Most MIDI sequencers and drum machines can store patterns on cassette tape. This is certainly handy—the data does not have to be manually reloaded. But cassette storage is inherently rather slow. This can especially be a problem in live performance. The audience does not want to have to sit and wait while the next song is being loaded from cassette.

Cooper's Song Store II speeds things up considerably, by allowing the recorded data to be stored on floppy disks, instead of cassettes. Floppy disks are much faster and more reliable than cassettes. A sequence that takes a minute or two to load from cassette can be loaded literally in mere seconds from a floppy disk. The Song Store II is priced just under $1000.

THE MIDITRACK II

The MIDITRACK II is a 16 track MIDI recorder/Synchronizer/MIDI remote control that is designed to work with all MIDI machines. It is marketed by Hybrid Arts, Inc. (P.O. Box 480845, Los Angeles, CA, 90048).

This is a very powerful and versatile digital recording system. All sixteen multi-function tracks are fully polyphonic and complete editing capabilities are available. Track bouncing can be used to extend the limits of the system. Overdubs may be made on any track. The MIDITRACK II has punch in/punch out capability with locate and pre-roll/post-roll. Real time, step editing, and recording are supported. Best of all, all editing is non-destructive. You are given the option of assigning the new version to the same or an alternate track. Individual tracks may be soloed or muted in real time.

The standard MIDITRACK II's storage capability is over 7000 events (notes, or whatever). This can be expanded to 40,000 events. Three sequences can be stored on a single floppy disk. All screen information is saved on the disk.

Recorded notes can be transposed in ½ steps up or down five octaves.

A visual/audible metronome is provided, along with an extensive multi-level synchronizer. Playback tempo may be varied over a 2 to 750 beats per minute range.

All functions are single key accessed for convenience. All MIDI modes and standard MIDI functions are fully supported by the MIDITRACK II. This powerful accessory currently retails at $350.

MODEL 242 INTERFACE

Sequential Circuits synthesizers can be interfaced with a Commodore 64 computer by using the Model 242 Interface. This device is manufactured by Sequential Circuits, Inc. (see Chapter 13).

This $99 unit is a hardware interface which is designed to plug into the Commodore 64's expansion port. It's features include;

- MIDI in
- MIDI out
- external clock-in (for syncing to a drum machine)
- footswitch in

Several custom programs are available for the system. You can also write your own software.

Model 910 Expansion Software
for the Six-Track Synthesizer

This software package is intended to increase the programming capabilities of the Sequential Circuits Six-Track synthesizer (see Chapter 13). Up to 100 Six-track programs can be stored as a group. This software also features programmable keyboard split, and front-panel screen programming.

Model 964 Sequencer

The Model 964 is a software sequencer that can record up to 8 different sequences with up to 6 independent tracks per sequence.

YAMAHA QX1 DIGITAL SEQUENCE RECORDER

The QX-1 is a digital MIDI sequence recorder manufactured by Yamaha (see Chapter 12) for use with their own and other MIDI compatible synthesizers. This unit is shown in Fig. 17-2.

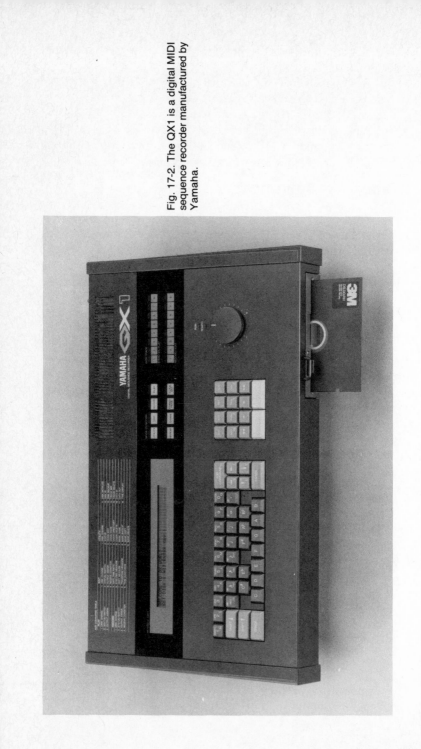

Fig. 17-2. The QX1 is a digital MIDI sequence recorder manufactured by Yamaha.

The QX1 features eight tracks and 32 banks. It has a built-in 5¼" floppy disk drive and can record more than 80,000 notes.

As you can see in the photograph, the QX1's front panel is set up something like a computer keyboard, although with fewer keys. The QX1 keyboard is divided into two sections. The left hand section is used to enter musical data, while mode and function switching is accomplished with the right hand section.

Data is read out on a two line alphanumeric LCD panel just above the keyboard.

Eight tracks of music can be recorded. Since only digital data is being recorded, infinite overdubs are possible, so there is essentially no limit to how many parts can be recorded.

The QX1 operates in four modes;

- RECORD
- EDIT
- PLAY
- UTILITY

The first three modes are pretty much self-explanatory. The UTILITY mode allows manipulation and examination of existing data. You might think of this as the "computer" mode.

The suggested retail price of the QX1 is currently just under $2000.

YAMAHA D1500 DIGITAL DELAY

Another accessory product from Yamaha is the D1500 Digital Delay, shown in Fig. 17-3. This MIDI compatible add-on is intended for use in reverberation and echo effects. A digital delay like the D1500 can also add a lot of lifelike quality to a pure electronic sound. A number of other special effects can also be achieved with a digital delay, they include;

- chorus
- doubling
- flanging
- slapback
- vibrato

The delay range for the D1500 goes from 0 (delay off) to 1023 milliseconds (just over one second) in 1 millisecond increments. In

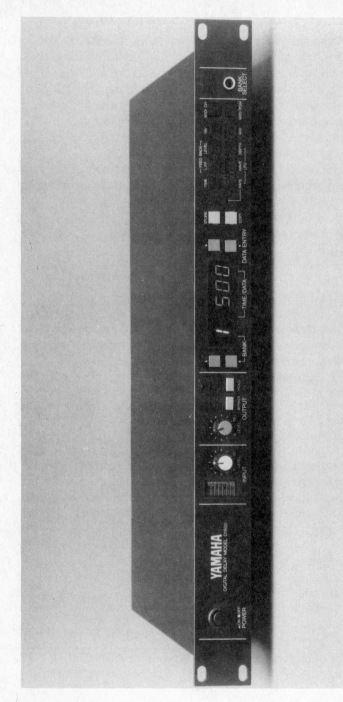

Fig. 17-3. The D1500 adds reverberation and echo effects to MIDI systems.

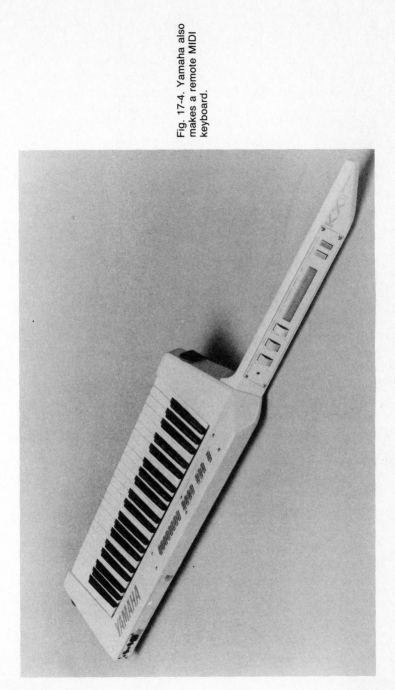

Fig. 17-4. Yamaha also makes a remote MIDI keyboard.

other words, there are 1024 possible delay rate settings. The frequency response of the unit is rated at 20 Hz to 18 kHz, so there should be no (or very little) audible filtering. The noise and distortion specifications for the D1500 are also exceptionally low.

The D1500 has sixteen memory banks for programming different delay settings. Programs can be recalled via the front panel, a foot switch, or remotely from a MIDI keyboard. Ten of the memory banks (0 - 9) are user programmable. The other six (A - F) come with factory preloaded programs, so you can get started right away—even before you have learned how to program the D1500 yourself. This $900 unit is apparently the first MIDI compatible digital delay system.

YAMAHA KX5 REMOTE MIDI KEYBOARD

Since MIDI compatible instruments can be controlled by an external, remote keyboard, many newer synthesizers are available with no built-in keyboard. This keeps costs down. You might want a system with three synthesizers controlled by a single keyboard. Why pay for two extra keyboards?

Yamaha also makes a remote MIDI keyboard. This is the KX5, and it is shown in Fig. 17-4.

This 3½ octave (37 note) keyboard is touch-sensitive. It offers full initial and after-touch sensitivity. These features are designed for use with Yamaha's DX1 and DX7 synthesizers (see Chapter 12).

The KX5 offers battery powered remote control of most important variables. It is shaped rather like a guitar, so the musician can play the keyboard with his right hand, while using his left hand to control other parameters, such as;

- modulation depth
- pitch bend (via ribbon controller)
- portamento
- sustain
- volume

The KX5 also features controls for selecting monophonic or polyphonic operation, recalling preset voices (up to 64), and transposition. The KX5 sells for about $500 and is available in two finishes, silver and black.

18

Electronic Drums

Playing a musical instrument by yourself is rewarding and fun, but it can be made even more exciting if you have some accompaniment. Generally, the best approach is to find a musically inclined friend and play a duet. This isn't always possible, or desirable.

In this chapter we will examine some electronic accompaniment devices to take over the role of a drummer. They have been called several names over the years—drum synthesizers, automatic drummers, rhythm boxes, drum boxes, etc. I feel "automatic drummer" is the most descriptive of these names. "Drum synthesizer" can be particularly misleading, since this term can be applied to an automatic drummer, or to a synthesizer to be played by a drummer, striking a special pad to trigger sounds.

Automatic drummers have come a long way in the last half decade or so. Earlier automatic drummers played perhaps half a dozen fixed mechanical patterns with five or six tinny sounding drum-like voices. On most units you could select one of the canned programs and adjust the volume and tempo, and that was it. The accompaninment provided by these devices very rapidly became monotonous.

Today's units really earn the name "automatic drummer." Some can do almost anything a human drummer can do, and a few can do some things a human drummer can't. Since I've never been very fond of traditional drums in the first place, I personally like automatic drummers that can play drum-like patterns in non-drum-like voices.

Most modern automatic drummers are programmable, so an infinite variety of rhythm patterns can be played. Some deliberately introduce a little slight imprecision into the beat, to create a more natural (human-like) effect.

E-DRUM

E-mu Systems, Inc. (2815 Chanticleer, Santa Cruz, CA 95062) manufactures digital drum machines, in addition to the Emulator (see Chapter 9).

The E-drum is a drum synthesizer, utilizing digital sampling technology. The manufacturer refers to this unit as a Digital Percussion Module.

It is a completely self-contained unit. Various interchangable sound cartridges are available to create different percussion sounds. Each cartridge holds one or two sounds in solid-state memory. A wide variety of sound cartridges are available, featuring acoustic and electronic drum and percussion instruments, and sound effects. Some available sound cartridges include;

- Acoustic 14″ tom
- Double snare (acoustic)
- Double snare (electronic)
- Electronic tom
- Gong
- Kickdrum (4 separate sounds)
- Piano
- Rock ride cymbal
- Rototom
- Snare
- Timbales
- Tympani

The E-drum is played by striking a drum pad which can be set to respond to the drummer's individual style, from the lightest finger taps to the heaviest metal sticking.

The drum pad gives the drummer control over the pitch and the volume of the sound. A decay adjustment and an active equalizer offer additional control over the sound.

External triggering may be used from a variety of sources, including synthesizers, sequencers, automatic drummers, or almost any audio source.

THE DRUMULATOR

E-mu Systems also manufactures a powerful programmable automatic drummer, called the Drumulator. This MIDI-compatible unit can store up to 10,088 notes, divided into 36 segments/64 songs. A song can last up to six full hours. That should be long enough for just about any musical application.

The Drumulator can correct timing errors as you program your rhythm patterns. The auto-correction resolution is adjustable for different effects.

The tempo is adjustable from 40 to 250 beats per minute. The tempo of each track can be programmed, along with tempo changes within the track.

Dynamics are also programmable on the Drumulator. You can choose normal or accented versions of every sound. Accented levels are independently programmable for each instrument. Different accent levels can be programmed for each stored song.

Any rhythm pattern—simple or complex—can be programmed in any time signature. Programs can be stored on an external cassette tape.

The Drumulator can sync to tape or other sequencers. It can be externally triggered from a drum synthesizer pad.

Twelve digitally recorded sounds are provided by the Drumulator;

- Bass
- Clave
- Closed Hi-Hat
- Cowbell
- Hand Claps
- High Tom
- Low Tom
- Mid Tom
- Open Hi-Hat
- Ride Cymbal
- Rim
- Snare

There are ten audio outputs;

- Mono mix
- Metronome/Trigger

- 8 individual instrument channels:
  bass
  snare/rim
  hi/mid toms
  clave/cowbells
  claps
  open/closed hi-hat
  ride

The retail price for the Drumulator is $745.

SEQUENTIAL CIRCUITS DRUM MACHINES

Another synthesizer manufacturer who makes drum machines is Sequential Circuits, Inc., 3051 N. First St., San Jose, CA 95134). (See Chapter 13).

The TOM is a MIDI compatible digital automatic drummer with eight digitally recorded instrument sounds;

- Bass
- Closed Hi-Hat
- Crash Cymbal
- Hand Claps
- Open Hi-Hat
- Snare
- Tom 1
- Tom 2

There is also a cartridge port for adding external memory cartridges with additional sounds. Each cartridge can add up to seven new sounds.

You get even more sound possibilities because the TOM lets you play any of the digitally recorded sounds in reverse. This probably wouldn't be of frequent use musically, but it can be useful for special effects from time to time.

Up to 99 rhythm patterns can be stored by the TOM. Each pattern can be from one to 99 measures long. All in all, up to 3000 notes can be stored by the TOM.

Rhythm patterns can be entered in real time or step by step. Once recorded, the patterns can be combined to create whole songs. Songs and patterns can be edited, copied and appended as desired.

Volume, tuning (pitch), and stereo pan can be individually programmed for each sound.

A five year battery can retain memory even when the TOM is unplugged. This can be very handy when transporting the instrument.

To avoid the mechanical precision of most automatic drummers, the TOM has a feature called "ImprovFactor." A series of "fills" can be programmed and automatically added to the basic rhythm patterns to create minor variations in the rhythm. The TOM also has a "Human Factor" mode. Minor variances of tuning and volume can be programmed into the stored rhythm patterns. The tempo is adjustable from 40 to 250 beats per minute.

Thanks to the MIDI interface, the TOM can be connected with almost any basic sequencer system. It has a multi-mode clock input and output for communicating with the outside world.

All drum parts, including volume and tuning, can be played in real time from any velocity sensitive MIDI keyboard instrument, such as Sequential Circuit's Multi-Trak, or Prophet T8.

Another digital automatic drummer from Sequential Circuits is the Drumtraks. It is also MIDI compatible.

You can store up to 99 rhythm patterns up to 99 measures long each. These patterns can be combined into up to 99 separate songs. A total of 3289 notes can be stored.

Drumtraks has 13 digitally sampled instrument sounds;

- Bass
- Cabasa
- Closed Hi-Hat
- Cowbell
- Crash Cymbal
- Hand Clap
- Open Hi-Hat
- Ride Cymbal
- Rim
- Snare
- Tambourine
- Tom 1
- Tom 2

These sounds are assigned to independently available output channels.

Volume and tuning are programmable. There are 16 values for these parameters.

YAMAHA DRUM MACHINES

Yamaha International Corporation (6600 Orangethrope Ave., Buena Park, CA 90620) also manufactures some state-of-the-art digital automatic drummers.

The RX15 Digital Rhythm Programmer is shown in Fig. 18-1. This machine, like most of Yamaha's current products, is MIDI compatible. The drum sounds are digitally recorded, using PCM (Pulse Code Modulation). Thirteen percussion sounds are available on the RX15:

- Bass Drum
- Closed Hi-Hat
- Cowbell
- Crash Cymbal
- Hand Claps
- Open Hi-Hat
- Ride Cymbal
- Rimshot
- Shaker
- Snare
- Tom 1
- Tom 2
- Tom 3

Fig. 18-1. The RX15 Digital Rhythm Programmer is MIDI compatible.

Each sound can have an individually programmed level, accent level, and stereo pan location.

The voices are stored in four 256K ROM (Read Only Memory) chips. If you are not familiar with computer terminology, K means 1024, so 256K = 256 × 1024 = 262,144. All this memory means the digital recordings can have a lot of detail for very realistic reproduction. The dynamic range is greater than 80 dB.

Programming can be accomplished in real time or step by step. Up to 100 rhythm patterns and 10 songs can be stored in the RX15's memory. The beat divisions can be up to 1/192nd of a bar. The unit comes equipped with 37 factory pre-programmed patterns already in memory. You can record even more patterns with an external cassette recorder for long-term storage.

The RX15 also features many powerful editing features. "Insert" and "Delete" controls are provided on the front panel. A single or multiple pattern can be repeated up to 100 times with the "Repeat" button.

Another control is labelled "Swing." This function creates a more human sounding rhythm by slightly delaying the timing of notes that fall on even beats. Most human drummers will tend to do this, so the result is quite natural. Each sound of every note can be programmed for 32 levels of accent or change in level.

Tempo can be changed at any point within a song. A LCD readout displays the current tempo in beats per minute.

The current retail price for the RX15 is just under $500.

An even more powerful automatic drummer from Yamaha is the RX11 Digital Drum Machine, which is shown in Fig. 18-2. It is essentially an expanded version of the RX15.

The RX11 offers 29 percussion sounds;

- 3 Bass Drums
- 2 Closed Hi-Hats
- 2 Cowbells
- 1 Crash Cymbal
- 2 Hand Claps
- 1 Hi-Hat Pedal
- 2 Open Hi-Hats
- 1 Ride Cymbal
- 2 Rimshots
- 1 Shaker
- 8 Snare Drums
- 4 Tom-toms

Fig. 18-2. The RX11 is an even more powerful Digital Drum Machine from Yamaha.

The various sounds can be routed through twelve standard phone jacks (¼") for individual instrument outputs, stereo left and right mixed output, or any combination of the two.

Rhythm patterns and songs can be programmed in real-time or step by step. Up to 99 patterns and 10 songs can be stored with up to 255 parts per song. Programs may be stored internally, or externally with a cassette recorder, or Yamaha's optional RAM1 memory cartridge.

The RX11 Digital Drum Machine is currently priced just under $900.

OBERHEIM DRUM MACHINES

As you can see in this chapter, many important synthesizer manufacturers also make one or more drum machines. Oberheim Electronics, Inc. (2250 S. Barrington Ave., Los Angeles, CA 90064) (see Chapter 10) is certainly no exception.

Oberheim's DX Programmable Digital Drum Machine is shown in Fig. 18-3. The drum sounds on this unit are digital recordings of live drums. Eighteen percussion voices are provided;

- 3 Bass Drums
    - loud
    - medium
    - soft

Fig. 18-3. Oberheim makes the DX Programmable Digital Drum Machine.

- 1 Clap
- 3 Crash Cymbals
    - high
    - medium
    - low
- 3 Hi-Hats
    - accent
    - closed
    - open
- 2 Shakers
    - loud
    - soft
- 3 Snare Drums
    - loud
    - medium
    - soft
- 3 Tom-toms
    - high
    - medium
    - low

Individual tuning controls for each voice are provided on the rear panel of the DX. Six independent voice outputs are included.

The DX also has a 7 input stereo mixer so you can mix the various drum voices, as desired.

Up to 2200 events can be stored by the DX's memory. Each event may consist of up to 6 simultaneous sounds. Up to 100 sequences and 50 songs can be stored. A sequence can last up to 5 hours at 25 beats per minute. The typical maximum sequence length is specified as 6 minutes of ⅛ notes at 80 beats per minute. A song can consist of up to 255 sequences. Clearly, the DX can play for a long, long time before you have to resort to reprogramming it.

Sequences may be recorded in real-time or step by step.

The tempo is programmable with each sequence or song. It can be adjusted from 25 to 250 beats per minute. Time signature is also programmable for each sequence. Step editing is supported by this machine.

Several Quantize modes are provided to correct rhythms recorded in real time. The auto-correction can be set from ¼ note to ⅓₂ note triplets. If you prefer, you can turn the Quantize function off for a more human feel.

A Swing mode is included in the DX to add the uneven feel that is often employed in Jazz, and other music.

This unit allows many special effects to imitate the frills played by a human drummer including changing tempos, flams, odd time signatures, off beats, rolls, and uneven phrases. Oberheim has gone to considerable lengths to ensure that the DX does not sound like an old-fashioned rhythm box. Their goal is for it to sound like an actual drummer. Programs can be stored in an external cassette recorder.

The Oberheim DX is no MIDI compatible, but it can be synchronized with some sequencers and other devices. It was designed specifically to be compatible with Oberheim's DSX Digital Polyphonic Sequencer.

Oberheim also makes the DMX Programmable Digital Drum Machine, which is illustrated in Fig. 18-4. It is essentially a more deluxe version of the DX.

Up to 200 individual sequences can be recorded and combined into 100 songs. The memory capacity is over 5000 events.

Some of the percussion voices that come with the DMX include;

- Bass Drum
- Hi-Hat
- Long Crash Cymbal

Fig. 18-4. Another Oberheim product is the DMX Programmable Digital Drum Machine.

- Long Ride cymbal
- Long Tom
- Rimshot
- Shaker
- Snare Drum
- Tambourine
- Hand Clap

Additional voices may be added with optional voice cards. Here are a few of the optional voices now available:

- Clave
- Conga
- Cowbell
- Electronic Bass Drum
- Electronic Snare Drum
- Electronic Tom
- Fat Bass Drum
- Fat Snare Drum
- Gunshot
- Noise
- Punch
- Short Crash Cymbal
- Short Ride Cymbal
- Timbale

An alpha-numeric display is included on the DMX's front panel, so you can keep track of what you're doing.

LINN ELECTRONICS, INC.

We have looked at drum machines made by synthesizer manufacturers, some manufacturers specialize in this area. Perhaps the most important such company is Linn Electronics, Inc. (18720 Oxnard St., Tarzana, CA 91356). Their LinnDrum is justifiably well known in the industry.

The LinnDrum is a fully programmable automatic drummer with actual digital recordings of all percussion sounds. The voices include;

- Bass Drum
- Cabasa
- Closed Hi-Hat
- Congas (2)
- Cowbell
- Crash Cymbal
- Hand Claps
- Open Hi-Hat
- Ride Cymbal
- Sidekick Snare Drum
- Snare Drum
- Tom-toms (3)
- Tambourine

Drum sounds are tunable by the front panel controls, or external control voltages may be used. External triggering may also be used.

The LinnDrum has a built-in 16 input stereo mixer with volume and stereo pan sliders and 16 outputs. The Drum sounds are user-changeable.

Up to 98 rhythm patterns can be stored by the LinnDrum. Programs can be entered in real-time. Patterns can be combined into 49 songs. Full editing features and adjustable automatic error correction are available. 42 rhythm patterns are factory preset.

An internal metronome helps you keep on time for real-time programming. Any time signature may be used. "Human Rhythm Feel" may be programmed in, or adjusted during playback. Dynamics for the drum sounds are also programmable.

An internal battery allows the LinnDrum to retain programs when power is disconnected. This is handy for transporting the unit without losing data. Programs can also be stored on an external cassette recorder.

A two digit LED read-out indicates tempo either in beats-per-minute, or frames-per-beat. The LinnDrum can be synced to tape, synthesizers, or sequencers.

The LinnDrum is a favorite among many professional musicians. It has been used on records by many popular performers, including;

- Prince
- Billy Idol
- Tina Turner
- Culture Club
- Michael Jackson
- Ray Parker, Jr.
- Miles Davis
- Hall & Oates
- Queen
- Paul Simon
- George Benson

and many others.

Recently Linn Electronics has released an even more powerful automatic drummer. The Linn 9000, shown in Fig. 18-5, is MIDI compatible.

The Linn 9000 is not just an automatic drummer. It is also a sequencer for use with any MIDI synthesizer. For some reason Linn Electronics refers to the sequencer section as a MIDI Keyboard Recorder.

According to the company, this is the first such combination MIDI sequencer/automatic drummer. Besides the convenience of having two units in one, the Linn 9000 is easy to use, since the operational functions are identical for both sections.

The Linn 9000's memory is expandable. Up to 100 synthesizer sequences may be stored. All standard MIDI functions are supported. The Linn 9000 can record notes played, dynamics, pitch bends, modulation, and synthesizer programs. It can simultaneously support up to 16 MIDI compatible polyphonic synthesizer units. 32 assignable tracks are used. Only digital signals are recorded by the sequencer, so there is no signal degradation. The performance is literally re-created during playback.

One very handy feature is that the digital recording section

Fig. 18-5. The Linn 9000 is a combination automatic drummer and MIDI sequencer.

functions like a multi-track tape machine. Of course there are Record and Play functions. There are also Rewind and Fast Forward controls to locate a desired point within a recorded track.

Keyboard tracks run parallel to drum programs. The Linn 9000 can be synced to tape, of course.

The automatic drummer section can store over 24000 events. Up to 100 rhythm sequences can be stored.

The automatic drummer section of the Linn 9000 can do just about anything other digital automatic drummers can do, including the LinnDrum. The Linn 9000 also has a number of nifty tricks of its own.

The Linn 9000 has 18 percussion sounds available;

- Bass Drum
- Cabasa
- Claps
- Congas (2)
- Cowbell
- Crash Cymbals (2)
    - standard
    - splash

158

- Hi-Hat
- Ride Cymbals (2)
  - regular
  - bell
- Sidestick
- Snare
- Tambourine
- Tom-toms (4)

All of the percussion sounds can be recorded in real time via a set of built-in velocity-sensitive rubber pads for completely spontaneous dynamics. The hi-hat decay is also programmable. These features simulate a drummer's variable pressures while playing, creating a much more natural sound. Rear panel inputs are included for external electronic drum pads, if desired.

The Linn 9000 features a built in stereo mixer, with separate sliders assigned to each sound. This allows selective memorization of volume and tuning. Programmable stereo panning is also supported.

The "Repeat" function permits fast, consistent programming of roles and other special drumming effects.

A 32 character alpha-numeric LCD panel acts as an information source for all functions in progress. The display is backlit for easy readability, even in the dark. This feature can be very handy for stage performances.

Another nice feature of the Linn 9000 is the HELP control. When activated, the advice relative to the current operation will be displayed.

The standard memory of the Linn 9000 is 64K. 64K and 128K expansion packs are also available.

Like most other digital automatic drummers and sequencers, programs can be externally recorded on cassette. Linn Electronics has plans to introduce an optional onboard 3.5″ disc drive for more efficient program storage and retrieval.

Some other options Linn has in the works include a plug-in SMPTE reader/generator card, an additional six trigger input card (for a total of 12), and a plug-in audio input circuit board for sampling (recording) new sounds. Currently, the suggested retail price for the Linn 9000 is $4990.

Software

A piece of digital synthesis equipment is nothing more than a special purpose computer. The musical applications are mainly in the software (programming), rather than the hardware (actual circuitry). Why can't a regular microcomputer be programmed for musical applications too? The answer is—it can. In this chapter we will look at a few of the many software packages available for turning popular microcomputers into musical instruments.

PASSPORT SOFTWARE

Passport Designs Inc. (625 Miramontes St., Half Moon Bay, CA 94019) is one of the leaders in MIDI compatible software. They market several software and hardware packages for Commodore 64 and Apple II (II+, IIe) computers.

This company was founded in 1980 by David Kusek and John Borowicz, who were certainly no strangers to the electronic music field. Both had been part of the design team for EML (Electronic Music Labs) one of the first commercial manufacturers of music synthesizers. Later they were two of the three founders of Star Instruments, Inc. This company developed the first computer-controlled synthesizer, and quickly earned a reputation as an industry leader in electronic percussion devices. The Synare drum synthesizer was one of the most popular instruments of its type.

While Passport Designs is closely associated with MIDI

systems, they went into the business of combining computers and synthesizers several years before the MIDI standard was developed. Their earliest products were software and hardware devices for creating music on Apple computers.

Their first major product was the Soundchaser Computer Music System. This was a complete package that included a music keyboard, sound synthesizer, and software for composing, education and recording. Some time later, Passport Designs teamed up with Mountain Computer for the Second Generation Soundchaser Digital System. Passport supplied the four octave keyboard and software, while Mountain Computer manufactured the primary hardware system.

At the 1981 NAMM (National Association of Music Merchants) show, Passport Designs was the only company to use a microcomputer as part of their display. They also announced a new software package called "Notewriter," which was basically like a wordprocessor for musical scores.

All in all, it is clear that this company has stood on the leading edge of the computer music field. When the MIDI standard was announced, Passport jumped right in. Their MIDI Interface was the first such device to be distributed on a national basis in January 1984.

MIDI Interface

The passport MIDI interface is fast becoming almost a de facto standard in the industry. A number of software developers and synthesizer manufacturers are basing their products around Passport's specifications. These manufacturers include; Casio, Korg, Lorev, Seiko/ Kaman, Wurlitzer, Yamaha.

Passport claims their interface allows you access to the largest library of music application software on the market.

The MIDI interface, which is available in versions for the Commodore 64, Apple II+, *II*e, or compatible computers, syncs to and from MIDI, tape, and drum machines. An interface of this type is needed to allow a microcomputer to communicate with MIDI synthesizers, drum machines, or whatever.

The Passport MIDI interface can connect an Apple or Commodore computer with 1 or more MIDI synthesizers, conventional or MIDI drum machines, and any analog tape recorder.

MIDI Recording Software

Passport also markets a pair of recording software packages for MIDI equipped synthesizers. These are the MIDI/4+ and the MIDI/8+. These two packages are essentially similar, except MIDI/4+ features four channel recording, and MIDI/8+ offers eight channel recording.

System requirements for use of either of these packages are;

- compatible computer (Apple II+, *II*e, or Commodore 64)
- Passport MIDI Interface (also available from Korg and Yamaha)
- 1 or 2 disc drives with controller
- 1 video monitor (or TV with RF modulator)
- 1 or more MIDI synthesizers
- drum machine(s) (optional)
- tape recorder (optional)

With the MID/4+ (or 8+), a single musician can compose, arrange and orchestrate complete multi-track recordings. It more or less turns you into a solo orchestra and recording studio.

The MIDI/4+ program serves as an electronic four track recorder. Track bouncing is supported for complex textures. For example, you could record up to seven parts with the following sequence;

- Record A on track 1
- Record B on track 2
- Record C on track 3
- Mix tracks 1, 2 and 3, and re-record on track 4 along with new material D
- Record E on track 1
- Record F on track 2
- Mix tracks 1 and 2, and re-record on track 3 along with new material G
- Record H on track 1
- Record J on track 1 and record on track 2
- Record J on track 1

The final track lay-out looks like this;

- Track 1—J
- Track 2—H & I

- Track 3—E, F & G
- Track 4—A, B, C & D

This is the same method used on traditional analog multi-track recorders, but there is a significant advantage here. On an analog tape recorder, the signal is degraded somewhat each time it is re-recorded. Distortion and tape hiss can rapidly build up to unacceptable levels.

With a purely digital system, like MIDI/4+, only digital instruction codes are recorded. The actual sounds are produced directly by the synthesizer during playback. Therefore, the sound has exactly the same quality, no matter how many times the material has been re-recorded.

The MIDI/4+ can drive up to 16 different channel assignments. Obviously, more than a single channel can be recorded on a given track.

The stored musical data can be entered directly from the synthesizer's keyboard. Just play your music, and the computer remembers exactly what you played, and can precisely recreate your performance at a later time. Notes and control changes are recorded as they are played. For complex passages, the notes and the control sequences may be recorded separately, then mixed together for automatic playback.

The tempo can be sped up without altering the pitch, or the pitch may be changed (key transposition) without affecting the tempo.

The system auto-corrects up to $\frac{1}{32}$ note triplets for perfect rhythmatic control. Over 6000 notes may be recorded.

All recording tracks are fully polyphonic. Virtually all controller data is also digitally recorded, including;

- aftertouch (pressure sensing)
- breath control
- pitch bend
- preset changes
- velocity sensing

MIDI/4+ also offers convenient editing facilities. If a note or measure isn't quite right, it can easily be corrected. The program offers features such as;

- single step playback
- fast forward

- rewind
- punch in
- punch out

These features combine to give comprehensive and convenient editing capabilities.

Looped tracks may be recorded and repeatedly played back as you solo over them. These looped tracks can go far beyond the capabilities of standard sequencers.

A drum machine can also be hooked up to play at any tempo set by the computer. In addition, the computer can produce a switchable audible click and/or a visual beat indicator during recording. The audible metronome signal may be fed through an external amplifier for greater volume than the computer's built-in speaker can generate.

The MIDI/8+ package is similar to the MIDI/4+ system, except it has twice as many recording tracks, making it powerful enough for most professional work.

MIDI Player

Another program offered by Passport is the MIDI Player. This package allows you to record your own MIDI albums (up to 8 songs per disc), complete with a high resolution video graphic display which responds directly to the tempo and pitch values of the musical score.

The program disc includes 8 pre-recorded commercial arrangements. The user can record original arrangements on additional blank discs. The recorded songs can be played back in any order.

Scoring Software

Passport Designs also markets several "score processing" programs. These allow you to compose and edit musical scores in a fashion similar to word processors.

Currently, there are two basic "score processors" available from Passport. The simpler of the two is called LEADSHEETER. As the name suggests, this program prints out scores in the familiar lead sheet format. Notes are printed on a standard Treble Clef & Piano score, similar to the scores found in commercial "fake" books.

Music is entered directly via the keyboard of any MIDI synthesizer. Notes are transcribed in real-time with auto-correction. The program can also automatically transpose the score to a different key than it was originally played in.

Once the music has been transcribed, you can enter and edit lyrics, chord symbols, dynamic markings, titles, or whatever you like on the screen.

When the score appears satisfactorily on the screen, it can be printed out on a dot matrix type printer with graphics abilities.

LEADSHEETER can correctly handle such potentially tricky score features as;

- accidentals
- beams
- flags
- note division
- rests
- seconds
- ties
- 8va's

Scores can be printed out in any time and key signature. If you need more complex scores than LEADSHEETER can handle, POLYWRITER should do the job. This program can print out multiple score formats with up to 28 polyphonic parts. Chords with up to 16 notes can be accurately notated by this system.

POLYWRITER supports virtually any score format you are likely to need, including;

- treble clef
- bass clef
- piano
- piano/bass
- choral
- piano/choral
- full orchestral score formats

Up to 16 staffs may be printed out on a single page. POLYWRITER offers all of the editing capabilities available on LEADSHEETER.

Passport Designs also markets a software package called POLYWRITER UTILITIES which allows you to combine

POLYWRITER/LEADSHEETER files with MIDI/4+ or MIDI/8+ for automatic playback of scores, or to include full MIDI information in the printed scores. This gives you a fully integrated music system with plenty of power.

LEADSHEETER, POLYWRITER, and POLYWRITER UTILITIES are all intended for use with Apple II+ or *II*e computers. For Commodore 64 computers, THE MUSIC SHOP can be used to print out musical scores.

Educational Programs

Passport Designs does not ignore beginners. They also offer several educational software packages in their MUSIC TUTOR series. This series is made up of three separate ear training programs;

- CHORDS
- INTERVALS
- RECORD KEEPER

Prerecorded Music

A rather novel set of offerings from Passport Designs are their MIDI SONG ALBUMS. Each pre-recorded floppy disc contains a collection of popular or classical tunes that can be played back in any order through a MIDI equipped synthesizer.

These packages may be used for instant accompaniment for jamming or practice, or you can just sit back and listen to the music.

Currently, three MIDI SONG ALBUM discs are available;

- BEATLES — a collection of their greatest hits
- POPS — current top hits
- SAMPLER — baroque masterpieces

Passport has also teamed up with Hal Leonard Publishing Corporation for a novel concept they call COMPUTER SHEET MUSIC. Each package includes a disk for an Apple II or Commodore 64 computer, and a big-note music book/user's manual.

The program is intended to teach sight reading and keyboard technique, while the score is displayed on the screen in large note easy to play notation with chords. Extensive use is made of color graphics. Notes change color when they are played correctly.

The melody can be played alone, or the computer can provide chord accompaniment. The output can be fed through a home stereo for high fidelity sound. The first COMPUTER SHEET MU-SIC offering is "Michael Jackson—THRILLER," featuring all the songs from the hit album.

DECILLONIX SOFTWARE

Decillonix (P.O. Box 70985, Sunnyvale, CA 94086) markets several musical software packages for the Apple line of personal computers. The package includes a hardware interface, software on floppy disk, and an instruction manual.

Any sound may be digitally sampled, recorded, and played back with the DX-1 and an Apple II computer. Sampled sounds may be played back over a five octave range. Sampled sounds are stored on floppy disks for convenient long-term storage.

Sounds may be sequenced in either pre-programmed or user generated patterns. Sounds can also be played "live" via the computer's keyboard. The DX-1 package comes complete with connecting cable, and 22 pre-recorded sounds.

The program employs the easy to use menu method. The main menu offers eight choices;

1. SOUND SAMPLES
2. PRESET RHYTHMS
3. REAL TIME PLAY
4. MUSICAL KEYBOARD
5. AUTOSEQUENCE
6. SCALE TUNING
7. EXTERNAL INTERFACE
8. LOAD/SAVE BASE

The Sound Samples section contains eight "demo" sound producing routines. Some of them have random features for greater interest. Any type sound may be manipulated and played by these routines.

The second menu choice is Preset Rhythms. Twelve pre-programmed drum rhythms are provided to turn the DX-1 into an automatic drummer. The user has control over several important parameters, including;

- direction
- pitch
- tempo
- volume

You are not limited to drum-like sounds. The rhythm patterns may be played on any sound.

The Real Time Play section allows the user to record or reproduce up to eight sounds, at the touch of the keys. This is one of several ways to play the DX-1 "live." The user has control over many parameters;

- direction
- memory format
- pitch
- volume

Another way to play the DX-1 live is offered by the Musical Keyboard selection. The computer's keyboard can be played live with over an octave of keys to reproduce any sound musically. The range is extended with instant octave and note transposition. The sound can also be played "in reverse" over a five octave range. The user has control over volume and sound recording features.

The Autosequence section allows you to use the DX-1 as a super-sequencer. You are given control over many parameters, including;

- direction
- duration
- memory format
- pitch
- sound selection
- tempo
- volume

Programmed sequences may be saved on a floppy disk for later reuse.

The Scale Tuning section allows the user to enter note values, tuning the DX-1 to almost any conceivable system.

The DX-1 can interact with the outside world. External triggering is supported. Input and output sync pulses can be enabled or disabled in the External Interface mode. Trigger and sync pulses are sent through the Apple's game port.

The Load/Save Base section allows you to load or read data from the floppy disks. Actual sound data is transferred in this mode. The DX-1 system sells for just under $350.

Decillonix also sells add on products for their DX-1 system.

DX-1 volumes 2 through 5 are collections of additional prerecorded sounds. They are sold together in a package of four floppy disks. Each disk contains a different sound category.

VOLUME 2—18 MUSIC SOUNDS, including;
    guitar
    piano
    saxophone
VOLUME 3—22 ELECTRONIC SOUNDS, including;
    explosions
    space sounds
    zaps
VOLUME 4—24 PERCUSSION SOUNDS
VOLUME 5—20 MISCELLANEOUS SOUNDS, including;
    car horn
    dog bark
    hiccup
    police whistle
    scream

The package of 4 disks sells for about $80.

DX-1 SPLASH provides a display of the digitized sounds in real time. Six colorful, key selectable, high resolution displays are available, ranging from fine dot patterns to oscilloscope-like horizontal displays. This supplemental software package currently retails for $45.

The DX-1 system's capabilities can be greatly increased with the DX-1 ECHO package. It adds real-time audio processing, echoing and reverb capabilities via over 40 key select routines. There is even a random echo length function. Controllable parameters include;

- end memory locations
- echo length
- echo loop start
- echo loop time
- sample rate

The DX-1 ECHO also allows joystick control of all parameters. The current suggested retail price for this package is $150.

The P-DRUM extends the DX-1 sound sampling system. Longer sequences, up to 3072 beats can be stored using the P-

DRUM. This can be divided into 48 patterns of up to 64 beats each.

This expansion software also transposes pitch and executes programmable digital delay functions. P-DRUM retails just under $100. MIDI-MADNESS adds full MIDI capability to the DX-1 system. It sells for about $100.

MUSICWORKS

Another company producing music oriented software is Musicworks (18 Haviland, Boston, MA 02115). Their software/hardware products add MIDI capability to the Apple Macintosh computer.

The MMU-501 MacMIDI Master Unit is a basic MIDI interface for the Macintosh. It allows simultaneous transmission and reception of up to 16 channels of MIDI data.

The MMU-502 Dual MacMIDI Master Unit is a more deluxe package. The MMU-502 includes two MMU-501 MIDI interfaces, along with provisions for drum box and tape sync. Up to 32 MIDI channels can be accessed via the MMU-502. Alternatively, the system can be set up for 16 MIDI channels plus drum sync in/out and FSK tape in/out.

Another product for the Macintosh from Musicworks is MEGATRACK. This is an N-track multifunction MIDI recorder. The number of tracks is theoretically unlimited because of the overdub capability. Since only digital data is recorded there is no signal degradation during re-recording. MEGATRACK converts the Macintosh into a powerful MIDI sequencer/ recorder.

The storage capability is determined by the memory available on your Macintosh. If the computer has 512K of memory, up to 36,000 MIDI note events can be recorded. For the stripped down 128K version, the upper limit is 6000 MIDI note events.

A particularly handy feature of Musicworks is the graphical editing facilities for individual MIDI note events. Each track may be given its own individual descriptive name.

Any number of MIDI synthesizers may be sequenced simultaneously. Other MUSICWORKS products include MUSICLAND (a set of four integrated music game/tools) and DX7 LIBRARIAN.

MUSICWARE FROM SEQUENTIAL

Sequential Circuits (301 N. First St., San Jose, CA 95134) is primarily known for their synthesizer hardware (see Chapter 13), but they also market music software. Musicware Model 964 is a powerful MIDI sequencer for the Commodore 64 microcomputer. Up to 4000 MIDI note events can be recorded, including velocity, pitch-bend, and modulation information. Full editing capabilities are supported, of course. The suggested retail price for this package is $99.

DIGIDESIGN

Another company producing sound synthesis software is Digidesign Inc. (100 South Ellsworth, 9th Floor, San Mateo, CA 94401).

Sound Designer is an integrated computer music system that allows the E-mu Systems Emulator II (see Chapter 9) and the Apple Macintosh computer to interface. Multiple graphic displays illustrate every parameter of each sound. Waveforms can be analyzed and edited. All sound files can be transferred between the Emulator and the Macintosh.

Digidesign also markets Digidrums chips. These are ROM chips for adding new voices to various popular automatic drummers (see Chapter 18). Drum machines supported include;

- Sequential Circuits Drumtraks
- Oberheim DX and DMX
- E-mu Drumulator
- Simmons SDS1/SDS7
- Linndrum

Most of the sound chips come in one of three formats;

- single chips that contain one sound
- single chips that contain two sounds
- sets of 4 chips that contain one very long sound

MUSICA 2

For a lower cost approach, you might try the Tandy (Radio Shack) Color Computer. There is a lot of musical software available for this inexpensive microcomputer.

MUSICA 2 from Speech Systems (38W55 Deerpath Rd., Batavia, IL 60510) is a powerful cassette based music editing/generating program. Up to four voices can be entered directly onto a graphically displayed music staff. Once a tune has been entered, it may be saved to cassette or printed on any of several dot matrix printers. Several popular printers are supported, or you can customize the interface to suit your individual requirements.

The editing capabilities are relatively extensive for a package this low in cost. Many handy features like repeats and numbered bar lines are supported.

Each voice is defined by a volume value (0 to 9) and 8 harmonics which may be individually set (from 0 to 9). Many special effects are made possible by the software. Several tapes of pre-recorded tunes are also available.

MUSICA 2 can sound particularly impressive when used with the optional STEREO PAK. This is a simple hardware interface (it just plugs right into the CoCo's program port) that allows the system to play through a high-fidelity stereo system. With the Stereo Pak, the music is automatically split into two channels. Voices 1 and 3 are played through one channel and voices 3 and 4 are played through the other.

Currently MUSICA 2 sells for $30. A 32K or higher Tandy Color Computer is required. The STEREO PAK (which may be used by itself, without the MUSICA 2 program) costs about $40.

Part 3

Building Your Own Synthesizer

20

Introduction to Projects

There are several good reasons for building your own synthesizer equipment. It tends to be a less expensive way to get your feet wet in the area of electronic music, and it can be a good learning experience. You can customize the equipment as much as you want, eliminating features you don't want and emphasizing those you do. Through customizing and experimentation, you can sometimes discover unique effects that aren't possible or would be very difficult to duplicate on commercial synthesizers. And, of course, building your own synthesizer can be a lot of fun.

In selecting the projects for this book, I based my decisions on the following factors: relatively low cost, distinctiveness and versatility, availability of parts and musical usefulness. With very few exceptions, all parts for those projects can be picked up at your neighborhood Radio Shack store. The parts that can't be acquired locally are readily available from some of the mail-order houses that advertise in the back of the electronics magazines.

Several of these projects are built around the popular 741 op amp IC. Whenever this device is used in a circuit, a dual-ended power supply is implied (see Figs. 20-1 and 20-2). Two 9-volt batteries are usually sufficient, but if you find they tend to go dead too quickly substitute a power supply. So many power supply circuits are available in other books that no space will be devoted to them here. Another possibility would be the small battery eliminators sold for portable radios and cassette recorders. These

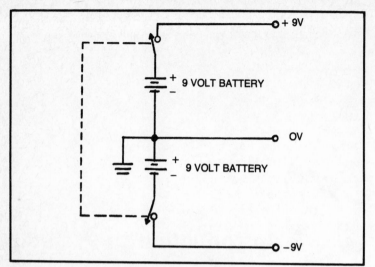

Fig. 20-1. A dual-ended power supply using batteries. The switches are two sections of one double-pole double-throw switch.

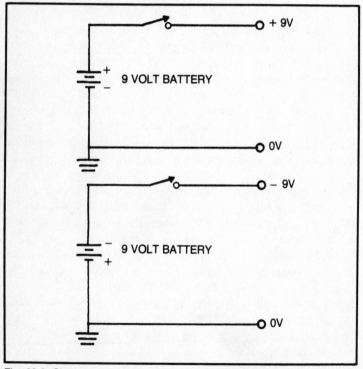

Fig. 20-2. Single-ended power supplies using batteries.

eliminators are available from any electronic parts supply store or department store. Just make sure it is rated no less than 9 volts and no more than 15 volts. Too low a voltage might make the circuits erratic, or not work at all. Too high a voltage could damage the ICs.

In all cases, include a power switch on each of the projects, especially if you're using batteries. To keep the circuit diagrams simple I have left off the power supply connections, but they must be included in constructing any project or there will be no way for it to work. If several ICs are used in a single project, they can all be run off the same power supply.

A pinout diagram of the 741, along with the closely related 747 and 324, is shown in Fig. 20-3. Note that the 741 and 747 require dual-ended power supplies, such as the one illustrated in Fig. 20-1, while the 324 can be operated with a single-ended supply, such as in Fig. 20-2. A 747 is the equivalent of two 741s in a single IC package; a 324 is the equivalent of four 741s. In circuits requiring several op amps, the 324 usually comes out the least expensive, even if one of its four sections is not used.

Other op amps could be substituted, but these three are usually the most readily available and least expensive. Their specifications are more than adequate for this kind of use. For example, the 748 is essentially a superior quality 741. Therefore, it can be used, but it will be more expensive and you probably won't be able to hear any difference in these projects.

Some of the other projects use the 555 timer (or the 556, which is two 555s in a single package) and TTL digital circuits. See Fig. 20-4. The power supply for these projects will be single ended, but it must be 5 volts. The 555s are pretty tolerant of voltage variations, but the digital ICs are not. Do not substitute a 6-volt supply, such as four flashlight batteries, without some kind of voltage regulator. A 5-volt zener diode could be used, but it would be better to use one of the voltage regulator ICs now on the market. Several of these IC regulators are available, and they usually come with a specifications sheet that tells how to use them.

In all cases it is strongly recommended that you use sockets with all ICs. Yes, they increase the cost of the project (sometimes the socket costs a bit more than the IC itself), but they're more than worth it if you ever do have to replace a bad chip. Desoldering and resoldering all those closely spaced little connections can be extremely vexing.

Unless noted otherwise, all resistors in these projects can be

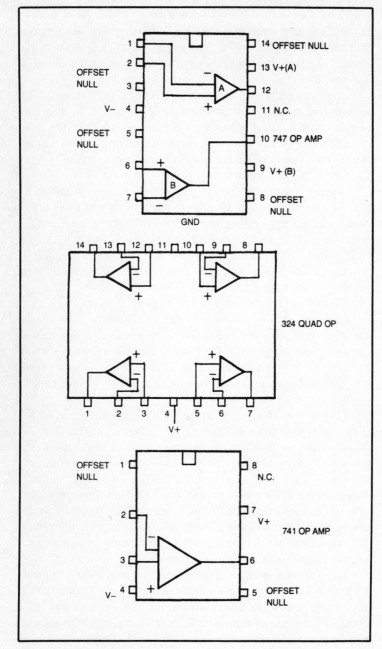

Fig. 20-3. Pinout diagrams.

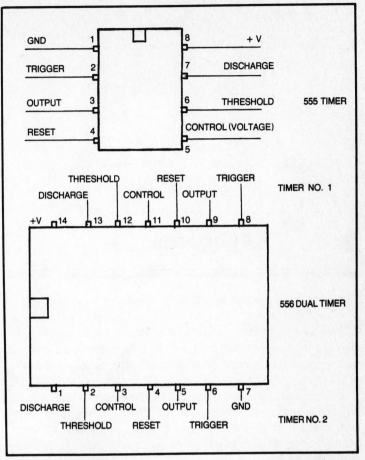

Fig. 20-4. Pinout diagrams.

either ¼-watt or ½-watt devices. The capacitors can be inexpensive ceramic disks or just about anything else you happen to have handy, unless an electrolytic capacitor is called for. Be sure to observe the polarity markings on all electrolytic capacitors.

Be careful to install all diodes, transistors and ICs correctly. It's very easy to install an IC backwards, so always double-check. If power is applied to the wrong pins, the Ic will be destroyed.

These projects can all be built on standard, fine-grid perforated board, or you can design printed circuit boards. If you use perf boards, you might want to use wire-wrap sockets or press-on, self-stick copper strips—at least for the ICs—to prevent shorts.

Keyboards

You'll probably want some kind of keyboard to control these projects. Of course, it's always possible to just twiddle the knobs, but it's hard to make music that way. The materials required for ribbon controllers are very hard to come by, and a sequencer would be a major project in itself, so keyboards are probably the best way to go.

A few manufacturers make complete keyboards that you can buy and wire into you own equipment. PAIA, for example, makes a keyboard and case kit. The price of these assemblies, however, is usually over $100, so they would end up costing more than the entire project itself.

Several options are still open to you. The easiest course would be to get catalogs from the various surplus houses that advertise in hobby magazines. Keep thumbing through them until you find a suitable keyboard at a satisfactory price. Some go for as low as $10.

Unfortunately, keyboards don't appear too often at real "bargain basement" prices. And when they do, they are often manufacturer's defects sold "as is." You have to gamble that you'll get a repairable unit. This gamble sometimes pays off with a super bargain when the problem is just a cosmetic defect, such as a chipped key or slightly bent connection. Sometimes, however, the unit is useless.

Cheap keyboards are often sold without switches. By the way, this isn't always mentioned in catalogs. If you use your imagination you can usually come up with some kind of switching system. One is mentioned later. Also, when keyboards are offered at bargain prices they almost always sell out very quickly, so be prepared for disappointments.

Another possibility is to salvage a keyboard from an old toy chord organ. In this case you'll have to devise your own switching arrangement.

You could attach a stiff metal strip of some kind to the underside of each key. These strips should be arranged so that they make contact with a sheet of copper-coated board each time the key is depressed (see Fig. 21-1). In this case, the copper-coated board is your bus, or common line.

Another possibility is illustrated in Fig. 21-2. Here a small hole is drilled in the rear of each key, and a straightened paper clip (make sure it will conduct, because some are coated with enamel) or other stiff wire is inserted through the hole and glued in place. When the key is depressed, the paper clip is raised and moved forward to make contact with a heavy metal wire or bar (the bus). Make sure that whatever you use as a bus will conduct throughout its length. You can test this easily enough with the ohmmeter section of any VOM (volt-ohmmeter). Just touch the leads to your bus at various separated points and check to make sure that the needle swings over to zero, or close to it.

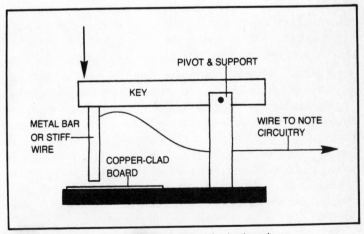

Fig. 21-1. A simple switching arrangement for keyboards.

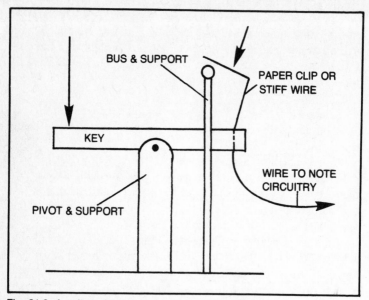

Fig. 21-2. An alternate switching system for keyboards.

Another way you could control your synthesizer is with a keyboard made up of normally open pushbutton switches. The main advantages of this system are that it is easy to wire. You can arrange the switches any way you choose if you want to avoid getting locked into the traditional 12-tone keyboard pattern. The disadvantage is that a panel of pushbuttons is difficult for most people to relate to musically. The second disadvantage is that good pushbutton switches are rather expensive, and you'd need two or three dozen. Cheap switches aren't worth the savings because they tend to be unreliable or get stuck, and generally have a short life expectancy.

A printed circuit keyboard is probably the best bet for most experimenters. Just etch a printed circuit in the ordinary way, using the pattern shown in Fig. 21-3. you can design some other pattern if you don't want a traditional keyboard. You then wire each of the touch pads to the individual note circuits, and connect a length of flexible wire to the bus point. Either tin the end of this wire or solder on a miniplug or banana plug. This keyboard can then be placed by touching this probe (bus wire) to the appropriate touch pad. This system is monophonic; that is, it can only play one note at a time. But most of these projects are monophonic anyway.

One last word on keyboards to the avant-gardists. Even if you use a traditionally styled keyboard, there's no reason why you can't

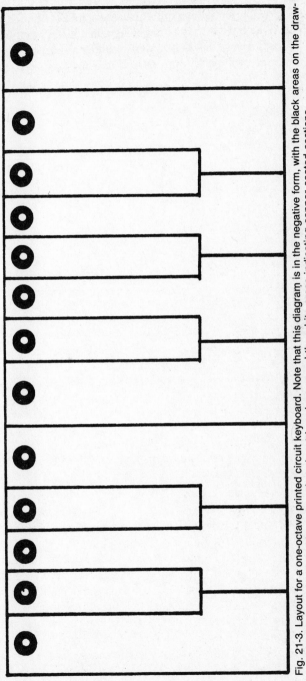

Fig. 21-3. Layout for a one-octave printed circuit keyboard. Note that this diagram is in the negative form, with the black areas on the drawing indicating areas where the copper is to be stripped away and the white areas indicating copper-coated sections.

183

wire or tune it to something other than the standard 12-tone scale. And you'll have the advantage of being able to easily notate your music. Just write it out as if it were traditional keyboard music. The hardware will neatly transpose it into any scale system you choose.

22

Op Amp Organ

Actually, this project isn't really an organ, but it's not really a synthesizer either. Whatever it is, it can produce some interesting sounds. It's quite easy to build too, so it makes a good starting project.

The Op Amp Organ is divided into four major sections as indicated in Fig. 22-1. The parts list is shown in Table 22-1. I'll deal with these sections separately so you can build the project in bite sized bits and test each section as you go along.

This project uses four 741 op amps, so the 324 quad op amp is a particularly good choice here. Remember to include a power supply, even though it is not shown in the circuit diagrams. You could use two 747s or four 741s, but keep in mind that you will need a dual power supply with those ICs.

Figure 22-2 illustrates a sample control panel for the entire project, and the Table 22-1 lists the component values. You can rearrange the positions of the controls, if you like, but be sure to think out the entire control panel before building any of the circuits to avoid problems in the final assembly stages.

After setting up the control panel, build the tone source (see Fig. 22-3). Connect the point labeled A1 to the input of an amplifier and temporarily connect a jumper wire from the point labeled A to the point labeled B. Don't worry about the pots labeled Rx just yet.

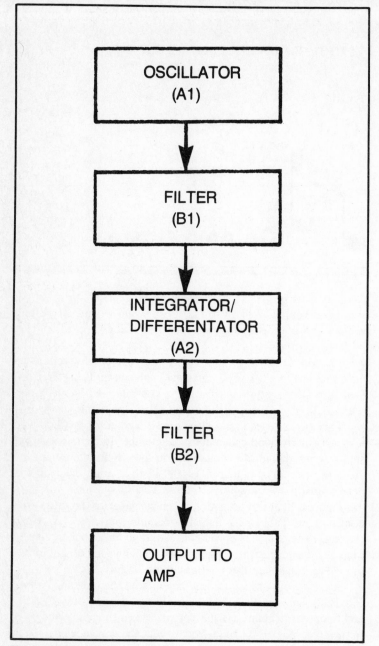

Fig. 22-1. Block diagram of the Op Amp Organ.

Table 22-1. Parts List for the Op Amp Organ.

R1, R2, R8, R9, R11, R13:	10K ¼- watt resistor
R3:	2.2K ¼-watt resistor
R4:	100K potentiometer
R5:	500K potentiometer
R6, R16:	5K potentiometer
R7:	270 ¼-watt resistor
R10, R14:	100K ¼-watt resistor
R12, R15:	9.1K ¼-watt resistor
C1, C6, C8, C9, C10, C15:	0.1 µF disc capacitor
C2, C11:	0.01 µF disc capacitor
C3, C12:	0.02 µF disc capacitor
C4, C13:	0.03 µF disc capacitor
C5, C14:	0.05 µF disc capacitor
S1 S2,S4, S5, S6, S7:	SPST switch
S3, S8:	SPST rotary switch
D1:	1N914 diode
IC1, IC2, IC3, IC4:	Op amp integrated circuits (four 741s, two 747s, or one 324)
Probe:	Miniplug
Touch-pads:	Printed circuit keyboard
Rx:	500K trim-pot (one needed for each note on keyboard)

Once you've double-checked for wiring errors and excess solder you can turn it on. Don't turn the volume of the amplifier up to high; the high harmonics created by this circuit could damage some speakers, not to mention your ears if you're not prepared.

You should now hear of sort of reedy tone from the speaker that will change in pitch as the pot is adjusted. If you have access to an oscilloscope, the output of this circuit will look like the trace shown in Fig. 22-4A.

If you don't hear a tone, turn off the power and carefully reexamine your wiring. If everything is connected properly, the most likely suspect is the IC itself. Pop it out of its socket and try another chip. Make sure the IC is installed correctly before applying the power (the power should always be off when installing an IC). It takes only a fraction of a second for an IC to be permanently destroyed by power being applied to the wrong terminals.

Once you have a tone, you know the main circuit works. The jumper can now be removed. Several pots in the schematic are labeled Rx. These are small trim-pots which are adjusted with a screwdriver. You'll need one for each individual note on the keyboard. I'm assuming you'll be using a printed circuit keyboard

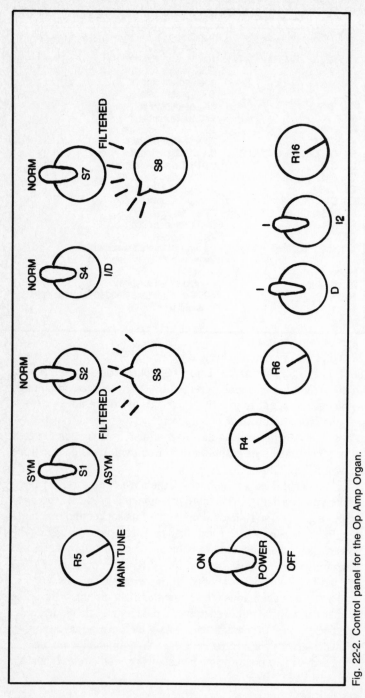

Fig. 22-2. Control panel for the Op Amp Organ.

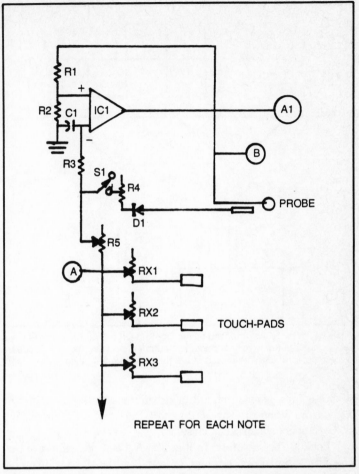

Fig. 22-3. Schematic of the tone generator for the Op Amp Organ.

here, so the keys are labeled touch-pads. Touch the probe (a miniplug) to each of the touch pads in turn and adjust the associated trim-pot until you have the desired frequency. Each trim-pot adjusts the pitch of just one note, but R5, which is on the control panel, raises and lowers the pitch of the entire scale. The individual notes, however, remain in tune with each other. Keep the trim-pots accessible, because they will sometimes drift out of tune and have to be touched up, particularly if the unit is moved around a lot. At this point you have a functional instrument, but the sameness of the tone can get rather boring pretty quickly, so we're going to add some voice-shaping circuits.

189

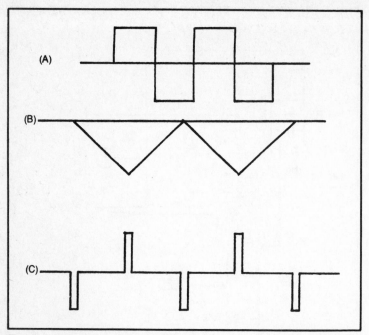

Fig. 22-4. Waveforms produced by the Op Amp Organ. At (A), a square wave is the output of the tone generator. The output of an integrator with a square wave input is at (B). The output of a differentiator with a square wave input is at (C).

One voice-shaping circuit is already built into the main tone generator. When S1 is open, R4 and D1 are out of the circuit, but what happens when S1 is closed?

Look at the waveform in Fig. 22-4A again. You'll notice that the output signal is either high or low. And the signal is in one of these two states exactly half the time. How long the signal is in each of these states is determined by how much resistance is in the feed back loop of the IC. If you don't know what a feed-back loop is, don't worry about it—just think of it as the way the frequency or pitch is determined. Because this is an AC circuit, the current moves in both directions. With S1 open, the current passes through the same components in either direction (R5 and Rx). When S2 is closed, the current will still go through R5 and Rx in one direction, because the diode will block the current in one direction. In the other direction, the diode will pass the current, and since R4 has less resistance than R5 and Rx, the current will tend to pass through R4 when D1 will let it. The high output and low output times will last different times, producing an asymmetrical rectangular wave. The important thing is that the overtone series will be different.

You'll also notice that the miniplug has two connections. The tip is connected to the output, while the sleeve is connected to the D1, R4 circuit. If you just touch the tip of the probe to the keyboard, D1 and R4 will be out of the circuit even if S1 is closed. If both the tip and the sleeve of the probe touch a touch pad, current can pass from D1 to the output and the circuit will be complete.

When you experiment with the tone generator you'll find that the pitch changes with the setting of R4. For instance, suppose S1 is open so R4 is out of the circuit, and R5 and Rx are set so the signal is high for .005 second. It will also be low for .005 second, since the circuit is in its symmetrical mode. Therefore, a complete cycle will last .01 second and the frequency is 1000 cycles per second.

If we then close S1 and adjust R4 so the signal is low for only .00025 second, it will still be high for .0005 second because D1 only lets the current pass in one direction. A complete cycle will now last .00075 second, and the frequency will be about 1300 cycles per second.

This is one of the reasons R5 is a front panel control—you can easily retune the instrument when R4 is changed. The Rx settings will probably have to be compromises (all of the notes won't be in perfect tune), but at most settings they will generally be close enough. Most acoustic instruments aren't always exactly on frequency either.

You can also use the this pitch variation as a special effect. Start playing a note with just the tip of the probe against the touch pad. Then tilt the probe so the sleeve touches the pad too. This will produce an unusual bent note effect. The tonal quality of the note will change too, increasing the effect. Notes can also be bent by turning the MASTER TUNE control slightly while playing.

The next section of the Op Amp Organ is shown in Fig. 22-5. This is essentially a very simple filter bank. When S2 is in its upper (NORMAL) position, the filters will have no effect on the output signal. When S2 is flicked to its other position, one of the filters will be brought into the circuit. Certain harmonics will be removed from the signal, depending upon the time constant of the filter. The time constant is equal to the resistance in ohms times the capacitance in farads, so varying the setting of the pot or the size of the

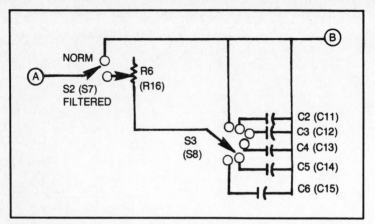

Fig. 22-5. Schematic of the filtering section of the Op Amp Organ.

capacitor will vary the time constant and the number and relative strength of harmonics in the output signal.

This is a passive filter so the harmonic content will vary through the scale. Unless the notes you are playing are widely spaced, the variations will be fairly subtle and not objectionable.

Nothing in this circuit needs to be placed on the circuit board. The switches and the pot are mounted on the control panel, of course, and the capacitors can be soldered directly to the terminals of the rotary switch. That way an excess of wires between the control panel and the circuit board is avoided. Connect the output of the tone generator (labeled A1) to the point marked A in the filter circuit.

Figure 22-6 shows the next section. Point B1 is connected to the point labeled B in the last section.

This section actually has three separate subcircuits, each built around a single op amp. If you look closely, you'll see that the circuit around IC3 and that around IC4 are identical. These circuits are called integrators. If you use a square wave signal, as in Fig. 22-4A, for the input to an integrator, the output will be a triangle wave, as shown in Fig. 22-4B. Using a triangle wave as the input will produce a sine wave. That's why I've included two integrators. Of course, other inputs will produce different outputs.

The circuit around IC2 is a differentator. A differentator is the exact opposite of an integrator. That is, if the input is a triangle wave the output will be a square wave. With a square wave as the input, the output will be a series of narrow spikes, as shown in Fig. 22-4C.

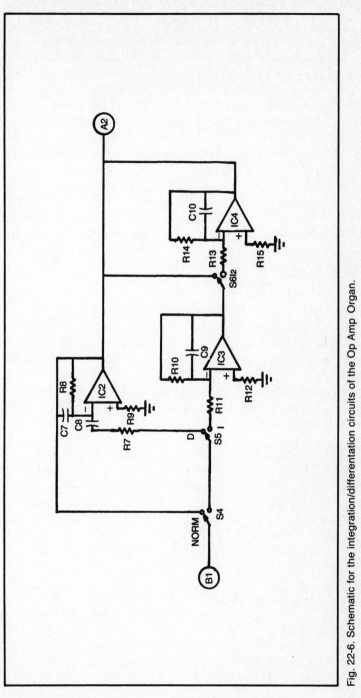

Fig. 22-6. Schematic for the integration/differentation circuits of the Op Amp Organ.

193

If S4 is in the raised (NORMAL) position, the circuit is bypassed and the signal is unaffected. But if S4 is switched to its other position, you can choose either differentation or integration via S5. There would be no point in using both simultaneously, because their positive effects would cancel each other. Finally, S6 lets you switch the second integrator in or out for further effects.

The last section of the Op Amp Organ is a repetition of the filtering circuit in Fig. 22-5. The filters will have quite different effects if used before or after integration or differentiation, so this simple circuit is worth duplicating.

Connect the point labeled A2 in Fig. 22-6 to point A in the second filter section. Point B of this second filtering circuit is the system output. Your Op Amp Organ is now ready to play. Remember, though, that this instrument doesn't even begin to approach commercial standards, but considering its overall simplicity, it's surprisingly versatile.

23

Digital Poly-Syngan

What's a Digital Poly-Syngan? It's a polyphonic hybrid between a synthesizer and an organ using digital gates. That might sound complicated, but this is really a very simple project.

Since this instrument is designed to be polyphonic, you shouldn't use the printed circuit/probe type of keyboard. Therefore, the keyboard itself will probably be the most complicated part of construction, and even that isn't too hard. See Chapter 21 for suggestions on keyboards. The keyboard for this project should have two separate sets of switches and buses, two switches per key.

Figure 23-1 shows the main tone generator for this project. The parts list is shown in Table 23-1. Using the traditional tuning system, this circuit should be duplicated 12 times: once for each note in an octave. Because there are multiple oscillators, more than one note can be sounded at once. Unfortunately, this also means that the entire instrument cannot be returned with a single master control, as in the Op Amp Organ.

The basic square wave generator is built around the 555 IC. If you use separate 555s, you'll need 12, of course. If you use the 556 dual timers, you'll just need 6. For the lowest octave, the output of this oscillator (point A) is connected directly to the bus via the first set of keyboard switches. The second set of switches will be dealt with later.

You could build a separate oscillator for each individual note on the keyboard, but that could get expensive and complicate the

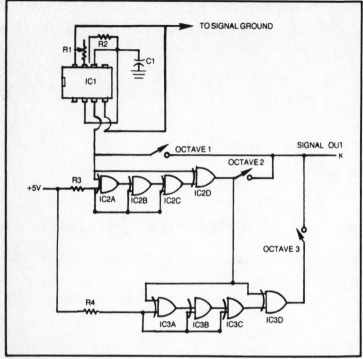

Fig. 23-1. Schematic for the main tone generators of the Digital Poly-Syngan.

tuning procedures. Fortunately there's an easier way to get octaves. Each octave is simply a doubling of the frequency, and this can be accomplished with a 7486 quad exclusive OR gate, as shown in the diagram. For the second octave, one frequency-doubling circuit is switched in (point B). For the third octave, a second frequency doubler is added (point C). Additional octaves can be added as desired.

Because each octave works off a single oscillator, they will always be precisely in tune with each other. All three octaves can be sounded simultaneously, so the instrument remains polyphonic.

IC1:	555 IC (or ½ 556)
IC2, IC3:	7486 Exclusive OR IC
R1:	100K pot
R2-R4:	1K resistor
C1:	0.1 μF capacitor

Table 23-1. Parts List for the Main Tone Generators of the Digital Poly-Syngan of Fig. 23-1. Twelve Identical Circuits Are Needed.

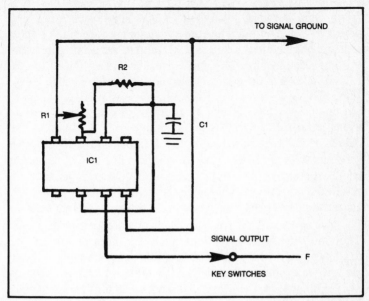

Fig. 23-2. Schematic for the free-running tone generator of the Digital Poly-Syngan.

Remember to include power-supply connections to each and every IC in the project. Since digital TTL circuits are used, the power supply must be 5 volts. Notice that the frequency doublers use the supply voltage as an input. This is in addition to the regular power supply connections.

Again, you could stop here and have a functional instrument, but the single tonal quality would get monotonous. So we'll build an additional, free-running generator, as shown Fig. 23-2 and a few additional circuits. The parts list is shown in Table 23-2. Notice that this oscillator is identical to the main oscillators. The switch at the output is the second set of switches on the keyboard. All of these switches are wired in parallel so that depressing any key will cause the oscillator to sound.

As I said, this project uses digital gates. A digital gate looks at two or more inputs and produces an output in response to the

Table 23-2. Parts List for the Free-Running Generator of the Digital Poly-Syngan of Fig. 23-2.		
IC1:	555 IC	
R1:	100K pot	
R2:	1K resistor	
C1:	0.01 µF capacitor	

relationship between the inputs. For example, an AND gate produces a high output if and only if both inputs are high. All other input combinations result in a low output. A NAND gate is the exact opposite. Figure 23-3 shows some of the typical types of gates. A 0 stands for a low signal condition and a 1 stands for a high signal.

If two square waves of different frequencies are used as inputs, the output will be a complex pattern of pulses. Some possible examples are shown in Figs. 23-4 through 23-6. K stands for the output of the keyed oscillators, and F is the output of the free-running oscillator. See the block diagram in Fig. 23-7. You should be able to come up with other possible gating arrangements.

In the diagrams it is assumed the input frequencies were 300 Hz and 400 Hz. Other frequencies would produce different outputs.

The two input square waves are of unrelated frequencies. Therefore, the sense of definite pitch will often be lost. In the examples given, the pattern will repeat with a frequency of 100 Hz, but some input combinations will not repeat for several seconds or even minutes, so there is on real sense of pitch. We consequently feed the gated signals through a mixer along with the unaltered keyed square wave. See Fig. 23-8.

By adjusting the levels of the various inputs to the mixer you can get some fascinating complex tones with the apparent pitch centering around the oscillator frequency. The harmonics, however, will be constantly shifting. If you calibrate the mixer controls from 0 to 10 (0 being off, and 10 being maximum), you'll generally want to have the main signal set at about 7 to 10, and the gate signals at 0 to 3. You might want to vary this relationship for certain special effects, but don't expect to be able to carry a tune.

The free-running oscillator remains at more or less a constant frequency. This means that tonal quality produced by the gates will vary across the scale. This effect could be minimized by setting the frequency of the free-running oscillator well beyond the range of the main instrument in either direction. The farther apart the two input frequencies are, the less variation there will be if one of them is changed slightly.

On the other hand, you could key the free-running oscillator just like the main oscillators, but tune them to slightly different frequencies. The disadvantage of this system is that it would be a major job to change the relationship between the two sets of oscillators.

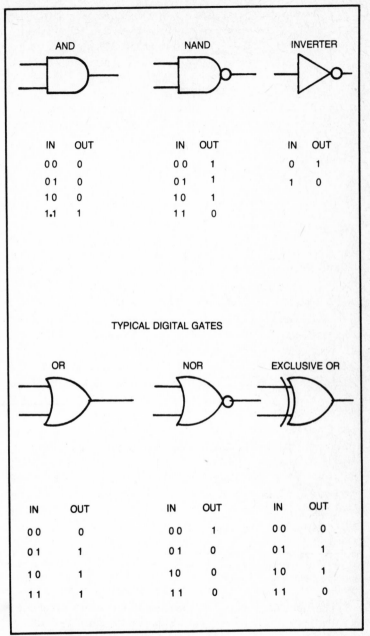

Fig. 23-3. Typical digital gates and truth tables.

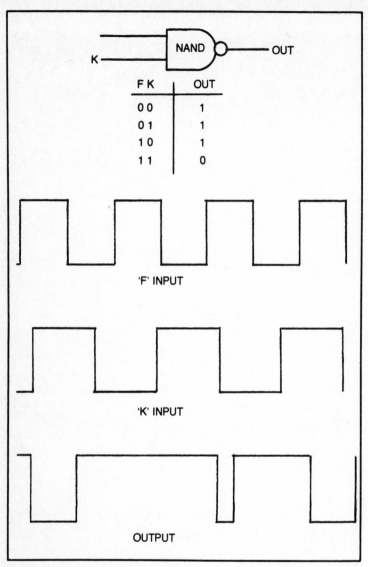

F K	OUT
0 0	1
0 1	1
1 0	1
1 1	0

'F' INPUT

'K' INPUT

OUTPUT

Fig. 23-4. A typical digital gate for the Digital Poly-Syngan, with its truth table and input and output waveforms.

The input switches in Fig. 23-8 could be eliminated to cut down on cost, but the pots by themselves may not be able to completely cut out an unwanted gate signal. You could also add one or more filtering sections like those of Fig. 22-5 either before or after the mixer. However, don't try to do any filtering before the gates,

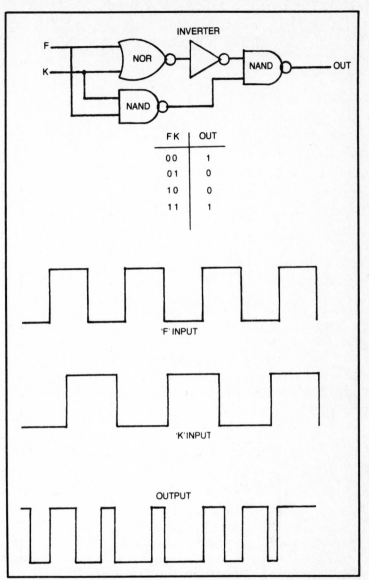

Fig. 23-5. A typical digital circuit with truth table and input and output waveforms.

because a filtered signal might not be able to trigger the gate properly (these devices are designed to work with clean square waves only). As a possible variation, you might consider including two mixers and have different combinations going to two separate speakers for a strange stereo effect.

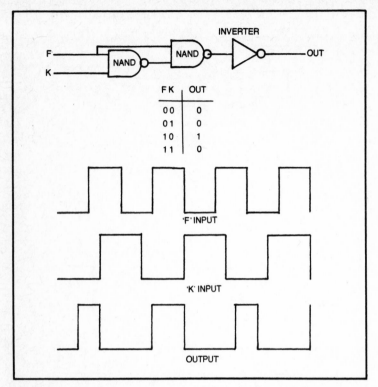

Fig. 23-6. Another typical digital circuit with truth table and input and output waveforms.

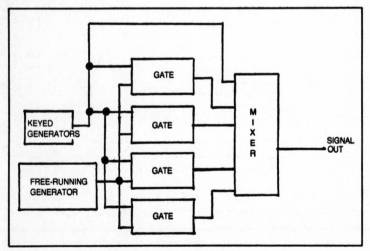

Fig. 23-7. Block diagram of the Digital Poly-Syngan.

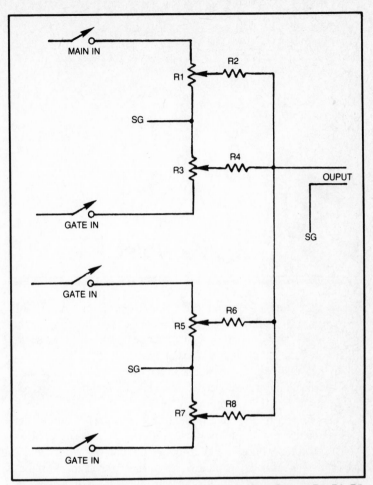

Fig. 23-8. Schematic of the mixer used in the Digital Poly-Syngan R1, R3, R5 and R7 are 1 Meg pots. R2 is 6.8K. All other resistors are 10K. More sections can be added as needed. Points marked SG should be connected to signal ground, not circuit ground.

203

24

Tunable Noise

We've used fixed filters in the previous projects. The cutoff frequency of these filters is constant regardless of the input, so the overtone series of the output signal changes throughout the scale. Each note has a somewhat different tonal quality to it.

In the Tunable Noise, we'll take a somewhat different approach: The source signal remains constant, while the keyboard controls the frequencies affected by the filter.

This project uses a noise generator for the signal source. The noise (a combination of all possible frequencies) is sent through a band-pass filter whose center frequency is determined by which key is pressed. The Q, or bandwidth of the filter is also variable.

The schematic diagram for the Tunable Noise is shown in Fig. 24-1. The parts list is shown in Table 24-1. Notice that this project calls for + 18 volts. This can be lessened somewhat, but the source voltage must not be less than + 15 volts or the filter might start to oscillate. Two 9-volt batteries in series could be used, or you could build or buy a power supply. Remember to include power-supply connections to the op amps even though they are not shown in the diagram. If you're using separate 741s, you must provide a ± 18-volt dual-ended power supply.

The center frequency of the filter is controlled by Rx. You'll need one Rx trim-pot and one Sk switch for each note on your keyboard. Notice that this method of switching in various resistances is essentially the same as in the Op Amp Organ.

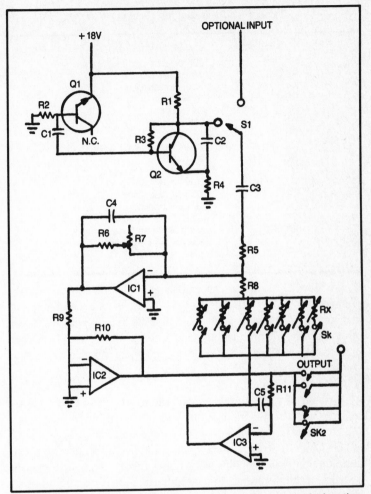

Fig. 24-1. Tunable Noise schematic. The source voltage must not be less than 15V, or the filter might start oscillating.

Therefore, the Tunable Noise is also a monophonic instrument. But a printed circuit/probe-type of keyboard cannot be used in this case because two sets of switch contacts are required for each key. The switches labeled Sk2 are in parallel and prevent an output signal when no key is depressed. Without these switches, the unfiltered signal would leak through when no keys are down.

The Q is adjusted by the pot labeled R7. When R7 is adjusted for a narrow Q, a very definite sense of pitch will be produced. Recognizable tunes can then be played on the instrument. As the

Table 24-1. Parts List for Tunable Noise.

R1:	100K resistor
R2, R3:	1 Meg resistor
R4:	100 ohm resistor
R5, R8-R11:	10K resistor
R6:	22K resistor
R7:	500K pot
R8:	2.2K resistor
Rx:	10K trimpot (one for each note)
Sk:	Key switches
S1:	Spst switch
C1:	0.1μF capacitor
C2:	0.005 μF capacitor
C3-C5:	0.01 μF capacitor
Q1, Q2:	Radio Shack RS2015
IC1-IC3:	Op amps (three 741s or three sections of a single 324)

Q is widened, the tonal center becomes blurred into a vaguely pitched hiss. If the Tunable Noise is used as an accompaniment instrument, it will generally sound like it's in tune with whatever other instruments are playing. One tone can be heard to be higher in pitch than another, but it's not at a single, identifiable frequency. Our ears, though, will tend to line up the sound to another simultaneous frequency.

Instead of using the noise generator, you could introduce an external signal. This input signal should preferably be a complex tone, such as that provided by the Digital Poly-Syngan, with a lot of harmonics. The exact tonal quality and overall amplitude of the output signal will probably vary noticeably throughout the scale because of the difference in passed harmonics. This might not be too objectionable in many cases, and the results can be quite interesting. S1 is included to let you switch out the noise generator when using an external input.

You could redesign a Digital Poly-Syngan and build in the filter section of the Tunable Noise after the mixer. A third set of contacts will be needed on the keyboard, and the polyphonic capabilities of the instrument will be affected. You can often ignore this and play polyphonically anyway. If other instruments are playing at the same time, the ear will tend to ignore the irregularities in the filtering. The Sk2 switches would not be needed in this case because the Digital Poly-Syngan already has a provision for preventing an output signal when no key is depressed.

25 | Applying Voltage Control

The previous projects have been rather limited because each individual parameter of the sound has to be varied through a separate means of control, and there are just so many sets of switch contacts you can put on a keyboard. The answer to this problem is, of course, voltage control. Unfortunately, most methods of achieving voltage control are rather complex and can't be retrofitted into existing circuits.

There is, however, a simple way to apply a sort of voltage control in place of any variable resistance or pot. This method is shown in Fig. 25-1. The lamp—a flashlight bulb—should be chosen so that the input voltage doesn't exceed the voltage rating of the lamp. You could protect the lamp with zener diodes as in Fig. 25-2, but generally you'd be better off just installing a higher voltage lamp. A 12-volt lamp would be more than sufficient for any of the projects in this book.

At any rate, the brightness of the lamp will depend upon the applied input voltage. The lamp then shines on the photocell, a special type of resistor in that the amount of resistance is determined by how much light is exposed to its surface. The lamp and photocell should be shielded from any external light source to prevent interference. A cardboard tube painted black on the inside will do the trick.

The end result is that the resistance of the photocell will vary in response to the voltage at the input. You can use either a dc volt-

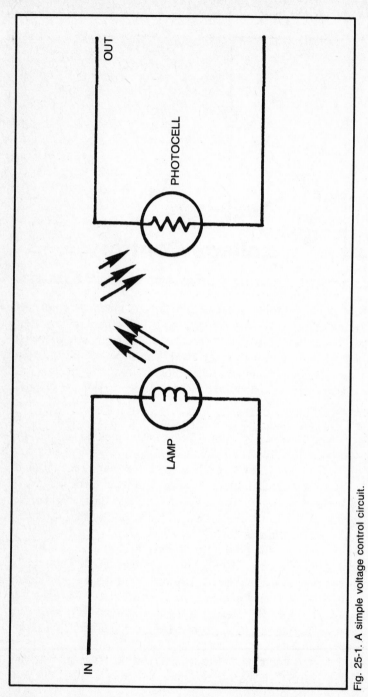

Fig. 25-1. A simple voltage control circuit.

208

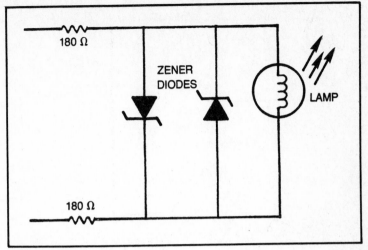

Fig. 25-2. Regulated voltage input.

age or the output of an oscillator as the input voltage. If you use an oscillator signal you should be aware that this system provides only one polarity since the resistance cannot drop below zero. Figure 25-3 shows the result. In most cases this really won't be much of a problem, and it can often be used for special effects. The photocell is useful in place of any resistor or pot in virtually any circuit providing voltage control to project.

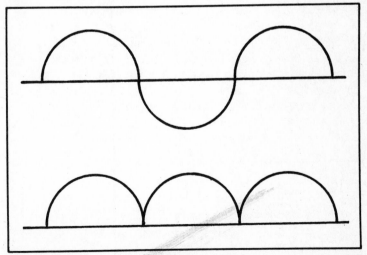

Fig. 25-3. A voltage control circuit has single polarity. A sine wave input would be distorted to look like the lower trace.

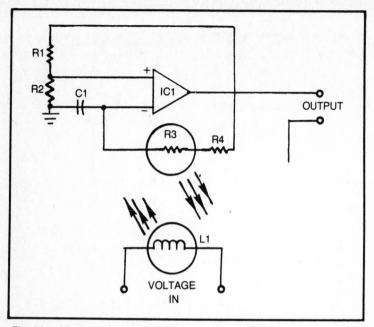

Fig. 25-4. Voltage-controlled oscillator schematic.

Now that you have a way of producing voltage control, you can build a modular synthesizer resembling most typical commercial units. Of course, the quality will not be nearly as good, the quality is quite adequate for a low-cost learning experience.

For a modular system you'll need VCOs (Fig. 25-4 and Table 25-1) VCAs (Fig. 25-5 and Table 25-2) and VCFs (low-pass in Fig. 25-6 and Table 25-3 and high-pass is in Fig. 25-7 and Table 25-4). An envelope generator is illustrated in Fig. 25-8. The parts list is shown in Table 25-5. This circuit includes a Schmitt trigger so that almost any signal may be used as a signal source.

A simple voltage control keyboard is shown in Fig. 25-9. The control voltage is obviously monophonic. The battery shown in the

R1, R2:	10K resistor
R3:	Photocell
R4:	6.8K resisoor
C1:	0.1 µF capacitor
IC1:	Op amp (741, ½ 747, or ¼ 324)
L1:	Lamp

Table 25-1. Parts List for the VCO of Fig. 25-4.

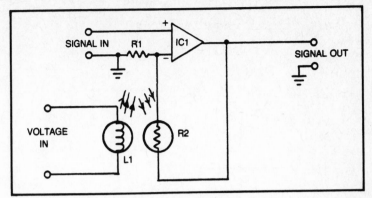

Fig. 25-5. Voltage-controlled amplifier schematic.

Table 25-2. Parts List for the VCA of Fig. 25-5.

R1:	10K resistor
R2:	Photocell
IC1:	Op amp (see above)
L1:	Lamp

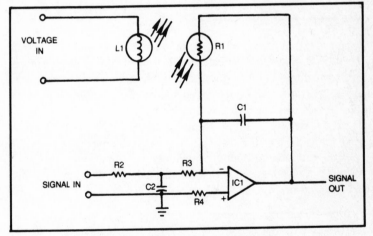

Fig. 25-6. Schematic of a low-pass voltage-controlled filter.

R1:	Photocell
R2, R3:	10K resistor
R4:	22K resistor
C1:	0.001 μF capacitor
C2:	0.022 μF capacitor
IC1:	Op amp (see above)
L1:	Lamp

Table 25-3. Parts List for the Low-Pass VCF of Fig. 25-6.

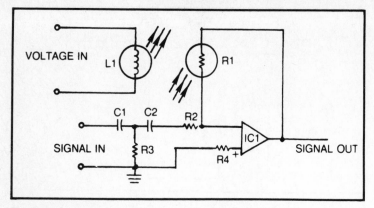

Fig. 25-7. Schematic of a high-pass voltage-controlled filter.

R1:	Photocell
R2:	10K resistor
R3, R4:	100K resistor
C1, C2:	0.01 μF capacitor
IC1:	Op amp (see above)
L1:	Lamp

Table 25-4. Parts List for the High-Pass VCF of Fig. 25-7.

circuit diagram can be of any voltage compatible with the rest of the system, and can be substituted with a power supply for more economical operation. Using these six circuits, you can simulate many of the effects of full-fledged synthesizers, including most of the patches described in the Appendix A.

The next two chapters feature some unusual accessories that can expand the capabilities of almost any electronic music system, even the modular concept-type commercial units. A few of these circuits can also be used with normalized synthesizers or any other amplified instrument.

R1, R2:	2.2K resistor
R3, R4, R5:	1K resistor
R6:	10K resistor
R7:	4.7K resistor
R8:	6.8 K resistor
R9, R10:	47K resistor
R11, R12:	1 Meg pot
C1:	0.001 μF capacitor
C2:	1 μF electrolytic capacitor
Q1, Q2:	Radio Shack RS2016 transistor
D1, D2:	1N914 diode
IC1:	Op amp (741, ½ 747, or ¼ 324)

Table 25-5. Parts List for the Envelope Generator of Fig. 25-8.

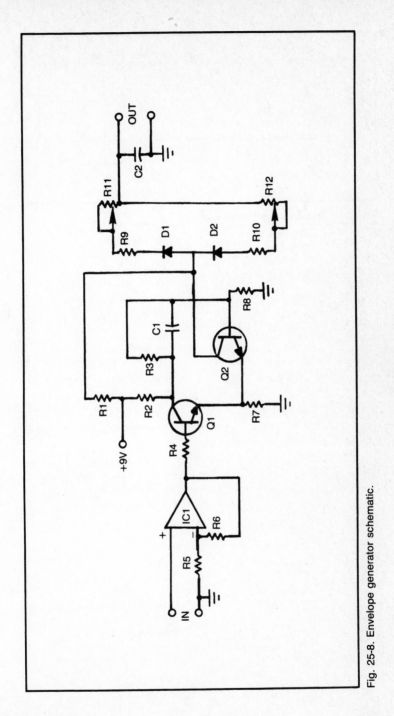

Fig. 25-8. Envelope generator schematic.

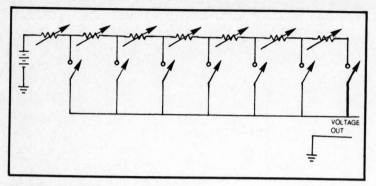

Fig. 25-9. Simple voltage control keyboard.

Modulators

In this chapter and the next, is a handful of miscellaneous circuits. You can use these to extend the capabilities of your electronic music system.

A modulator is a device that modulates, or changes, a signal in some way. In other words, the output is different from the input. A filter is a common type of modulator.

The circuit in Fig. 26-1 produces two outputs from a single input. The parts list is shown in Table 26-1. One output is a sawtooth wave; the other is a rectangular wave. The frequency and phase of these two outputs will be identical, and it will be determined by the voltage at the input. Actually, this circuit isn't as much a modulator as it is a VCO, but a VCO can be used as a sort of modulator if the input frequency is in the audio range of frequencies.

A simple single input modulator is shown in Fig. 26-2. The parts list is shown in Table 26-2. This circuit is designed to produce a clean sine wave output from a triangle wave input. Other inputs will produce different outputs, of course.

Essentially, this circuit is an integrator, similar in function to the one in Chapter 22. This one, though, provides somewhat better linearity, or smoothness of output. This circuit can be substituted for the integrators in the Op Amp Organ, or it can be used at the output of almost any electronic instrument. The effect is most noticeable on fairly simple waveforms.

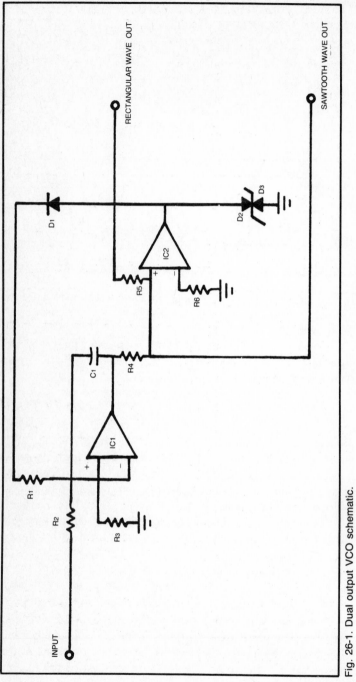

Fig. 26-1. Dual output VCO schematic.

216

Table 26-1. Parts List of the Dual Output VCO of Fig. 26-1.

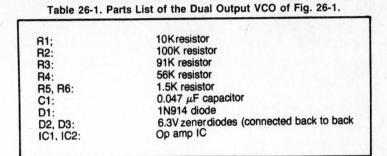

R1;	10K resistor
R2:	100K resistor
R3:	91K resistor
R4:	56K resistor
R5, R6:	1.5K resistor
C1:	0.047 μF capacitor
D1:	1N914 diode
D2, D3:	6.3V zener diodes (connected back to back
IC1, IC2:	Op amp IC

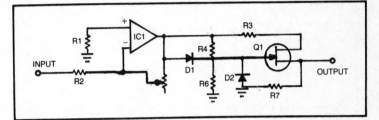

Fig. 26-2. Integrator schematic.

Table 26-2. Parts List of the Integrator of Fig. 26-2.

R1, R2:	10K resistor
R3, R7:	100 ohm resistor
R4, R6:	1 Meg resistor
R5:	50K pot
D1, D2:	1N914 diode
Q1:	Radio Shack RS 2037 FET
IC1:	Op amp

In Fig. 26-3 we're getting into a more advanced breed of modulators with two inputs rather than just one. One input will modulate the way the other input signal will appear at the output. The parts list for this circuit is shown in Table 26-3.

This particular circuit is a differentiator, as in Chapter 22. But this is a differentiator with a difference. This circuit will subtract one of the inputs from the other (see Fig. 26-4) and differentiates the result. This can produce some very novel sounds.

The input is not limited to square waves. Further variations can be achieved by adjusting one or both of the 500-ohm input pots.

A staircase wave can be produced with the circuit shown in Fig. 26-5. The parts list is shown in Table 26-4. A square wave is applied to the input. Another rectangular wave is used as the trigger source. The input should be at least twice the trigger

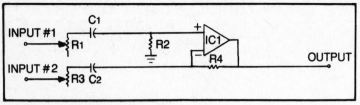

Fig. 26-3. Differential differentiator.

R1, R3:	500Ω pots
R2, R4:	10K resistor
C1, C2:	0.1 μF capacitor
IC1:	Op amp

Table 26-3. Parts List of the Differential Differentiator of Fig. 26-3.

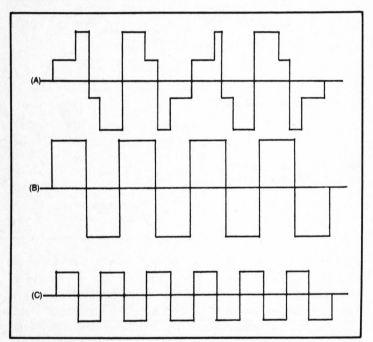

Fig. 26-4. The waveform of (A) is the result of subtracting the waveform of (C) from that of (B).

frequency and preferably more. The frequency of the staircase wave will be equal to that of the trigger. The steps will be equal to the frequency and amplitude of input signal. See Fig. 26-6 for sample waveforms. If the trigger frequency is considerably higher than the input frequency, the output will sound roughly like an ascending sawtooth wave.

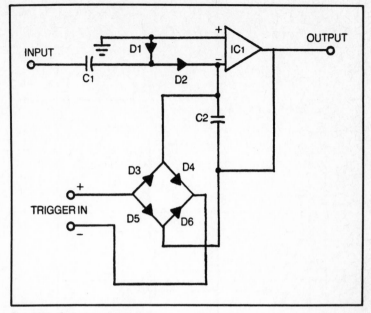

Fig. 26-5. Staircase generator.

The circuit in Fig. 26-7 is a phase shifter. The parts list is shown in Table 26-5. See also Fig. 26-8. By itself the output of this device won't sound any different than the input. But if the output of the phase shifter is fed through a mixer along with the unshifted input signal, a shifting chorus-like tone will be heard. This will also produce sidebands because sometimes the two signals will cancel each other, and other times they will reinforce each other, producing a form of amplitude modulation.

Adjusting one or both of the pots while the tone is sounding will greatly increase the shifting quality of the effect. In fact, this is an excellent circuit to adapt for voltage-controlled operation. The result will be similar to the Flangers that are popular with guitarists.

I did not include the mixer in the basic circuit, because it is often desirable to feed the shifted and unshifted signals through

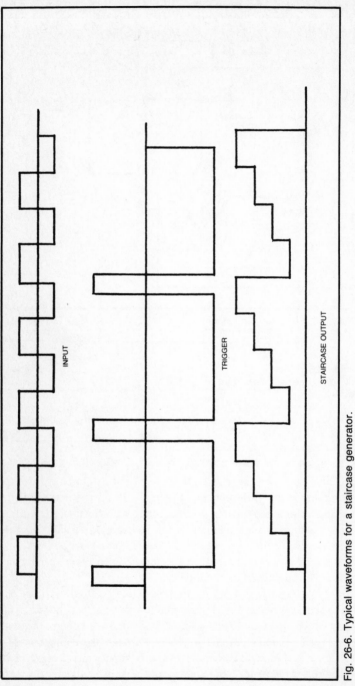

INPUT

TRIGGER

STAIRCASE OUTPUT

Fig. 26-6. Typical waveforms for a staircase generator.

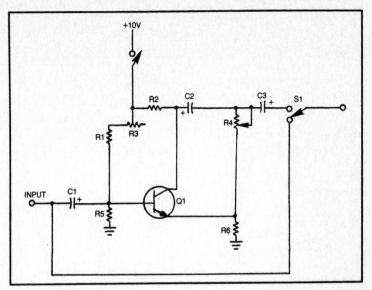

Fig. 26-7. Phase shifter.

Table 26-5. Parts List of the Phase Shifter of Fig. 26-7.

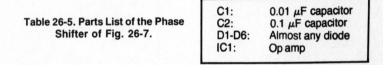

C1:	0.01 μF capacitor
C2:	0.1 μF capacitor
D1-D6:	Almost any diode
IC1:	Op amp

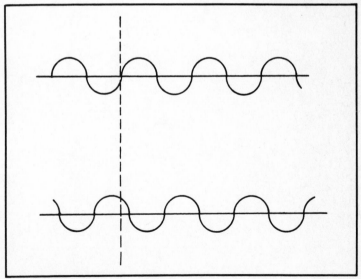

Fig. 26-8. Signals that are out of phase with each other.

different modulators before mixing them. The switch is to give you an easy and quick way to cut the effect in and out of the patch while playing. Mixing the input signal with itself will produce no audible effect.

For a full chorus effect you can use three or four phase shifters simultaneously. Each shifter should be set slightly differently than all the others. This effect tends to work better with relatively simply waveforms. With a complex signal as the input, the sidebands in the output will tend to blur and produce a sound similar to white noise.

27

Drones

A drone is a more or less continuous tone that does not sound separate discernible notes. It can be mixed with the main output at a much lower level to add more body to the total sound. This approach is used in the Digital Poly-Syngan. Drones can also be used as the second input in a modulator, or as a source of repeating voltage controls. Complex waveforms are best suited for the first application, while fairly simple waveforms are better for the second.

Figures 27-1 and 27-2 show two simple drones. These are simply oscillators. Figure 27-1 is the same variable-width rectangular wave generator used in the Op Amp Organ. The circuit in Fig. 27-2 is a sine wave oscillator. Notice that two parts lists for this circuit are included to allow two different frequency ranges. These lists are shown in Tables 27-2 and 27-3.

You could also use the free-running oscillator from the Digital Poly-Syngan (Chapter 23) as a drone source. For a more complex drone you can feed two or more of these oscillators through digital gates, as outlined in Chapter 14. The indefinite sense of pitch these gates provide would make this an ideal accompaniment drone.

Do not, however, use Op Amp oscillators as inputs to digital gates. The difference in voltage levels could possibly damage the gates.

Another good way to achieve a complex drone is to mix together several simple drones of slightly different frequencies and maybe put a filter at the output. The passive filter in Chapter 13 would

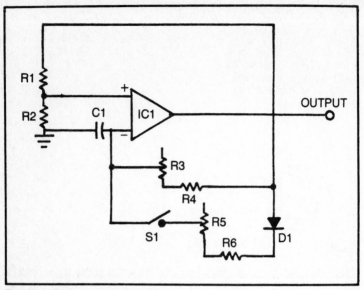

Fig. 27-1. Square wave generator.

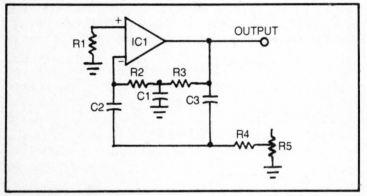

Fig. 27-2. Sine wave oscillator.

R1, R2:	10K resistor
R3:	500K pot
R4:	100K resistor
R5:	100K pot
R6:	47K resistor
C1:	0.1 μF capacitor
D1:	1N914 diode
IC1:	OP amp IC
S1:	Spst switch

Table 27-1.
Parts List for the Square
Wave Generator of Fig. 27-1.

R1:	22K resistor
R2, R3:	10K resistor
R4:	2.7K resistor
R5:	5K pot
C1:	4.7 μF capacitor
C2, C3:	2.2 μF capacitor
IC1:	Op amp IC

Table 27-2. Parts List for the Low-Frequency Sine Wave Oscillator of Fig. 27-2.

be fine. If the source frequencies are very close to each other, FM sidebands will be produced.

For a continuously variable effect, you could use joystick-type potentiometers to control the frequency of the oscillators and the input levels of the mixer. Joysticks are available from many of the mail-order surplus houses.

This type of drone usually sounds the best if sine wave oscillators are used as the input sources, but more complex waveforms can be used occasionally for special effects. Figure 27-3 shows a block diagram for this system. Of course, you can adapt it to suit your individual purposes. You could use the passive mixer shown in Chapter 23, but to avoid loss in signal strength you could use the active mixer shown in Fig. 27-4. Only two inputs are shown, but more could be added as desired.

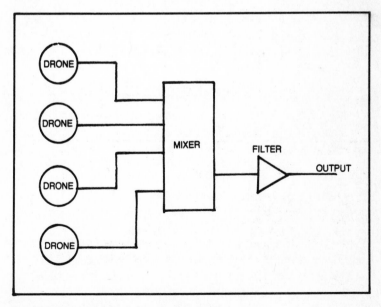

Fig. 27-3. Block diagram of a complex drone.

R1:	4.7K resistor
R2, R3:	2.2K resistor
R4:	560 ohm resistor
R5:	1K pot
C1:	0.22 µF capacitor
C2, C3:	0.1 µF capacitor
IC1	Op amp IC

Table 27-3. Parts List for the Midrange Frequency Sine Wave Oscillator of Fig. 27-2.

Table 27-4. Parts List for the Active Mixer of Fig. 27-4.

R1:	100K resistor*
R2:	10K pot*
IC1:	op amp IC*
IC2:	op amp IC
R3:	100K resistor
R4:	22K resistor
*Repeated for each input.	

This active mixer could also be substituted for the passive mixer called for in the Digital Poly-Syngan, but remember that the op amps require at least 9 volts, while the digital circuits can't take more than 5 volts without damage. A 555 will work on either 5 or 9 volts.

Let's close with a novel little circuit I call the Fall and Bounce (see Fig. 27-5). When the pushbutton is momentarily depressed, C1 is allowed to discharge. When the switch is released, this capacitor is charged through the transistor and produces a descending pitch whistling tone. If S1 is not depressed again, a series of widely separated pulses will sound. This is caused by leakage in the capacitor.

The whistle sounds like the sound effects used in cartoons to accompany a falling object. The isolated pulses afterwards suggest that the object is bouncing. The pulses are of a much lower amplitude than the whistle, so in many applications they can be ignored.

The frequency range of the whistle is set by R1, and the length of the whistle can be changed by substituting different values for C1. The larger the capacitance, the longer the whistle is.

Feel free to experiment with any or all of these circuits. You'll soon discover that it's really not very hard to come up with unique variations of your own. And producing unique new sounds is what electronic music is all about.

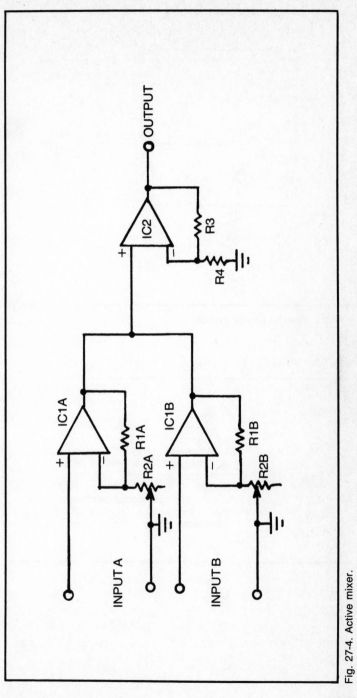

Fig. 27-4. Active mixer.

227

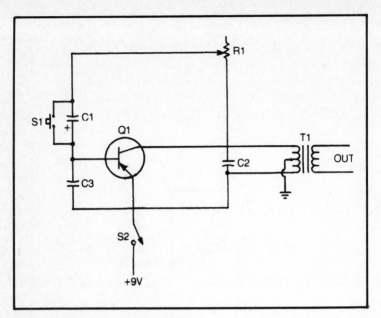

Fig. 27-5. Fall and Bounce schematic.

Table 27-5. Parts List for the Fall and Bounce of Fig. 27-5.

R1:	250K pot
C1:	10µF electrolytic capacitor (see text)
C2:	0.1 µF capacitor
C3:	0.01 µF capacitor
Q1:	Radio Shack RS2003 transistor (PNP)
S1:	Normally open spst pushbutton switch
S2:	Spst switch
T1:	Almost any audio frequency transformer—impedance ratio should be about 2500:600Ω but this is not terribly critical.

Appendix A
Universal Patch Diagrams

What follows is a collection of sample patches in universal form. Not all of the patches shown will be possible on all synthesizers, and some might sound absolutely terrible on certain units. These sample patches are to serve only as a springboard for your imagination.

These patches are based on standard analog synthesis modules. They can be used on digital synthesizers that emulate analog equipment. Unfortunately, there is no standardization at all when it comes to purely digital techniques, so only analog-type patches are illustrated here.

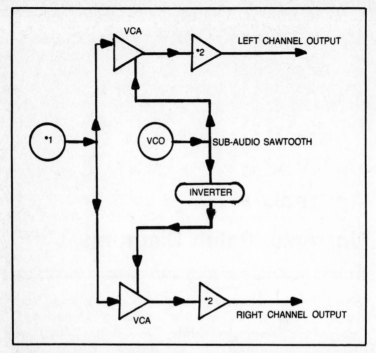

Fig. A-1. *1 can be any source. *2 signifies further processing as desired. This patch will cause the signal to pan from one output to the other, and then snap back to its starting point and start over. Other waveshapes can also be used. If the output of the VCO is brought up into the audible region, the sound will appear to come from somewhere in between the speakers, and sidebands will be produced.

Fig. A-2. This patch gives a sliding chord effect. One tone emerges from another. Settings are as follows: VCO No. 1 is the fundamental frequency (eg., C); VCO No 2. is the fundamental's third (eg., E); and VCO No. 3 is the fundamental's fifth (eg., G). Other intervals could be used for different chords. FG No. 1 is set for medium fast attack/medium slow decay. FG No. 2 is set for medium slow attack/medium slow decay. And FG No. 3 is set for medium slow attack/medium fast decay. All mixer inputs should be kept about equal, although you might want to boost up the gain of the fundamental (VCO No. 1) just a little. T stands for trigger, and all these points should be tied together. Sustain on the function generators may or may not be used, depending on the music being played. You might want to use sustain on one of the tones—probably the fundamental—and not on the other notes.

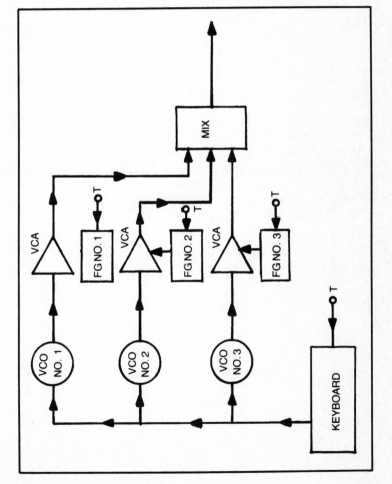

231

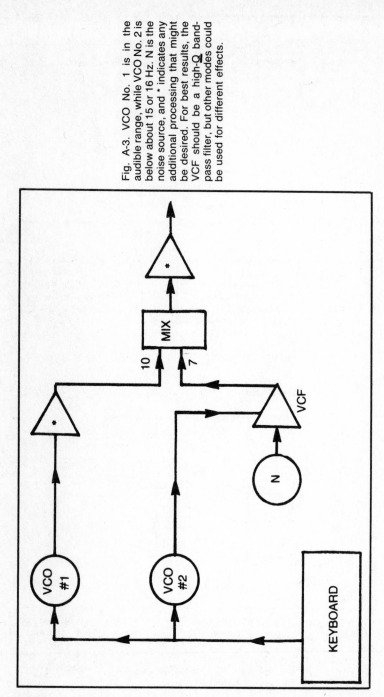

Fig. A-3. VCO No. 1 is in the audible range, while VCO No. 2 is below about 15 or 16 Hz. N is the noise source, and * indicates any additional processing that might be desired. For best results, the VCF should be a high-Q band-pass filter, but other modes could be used for different effects.

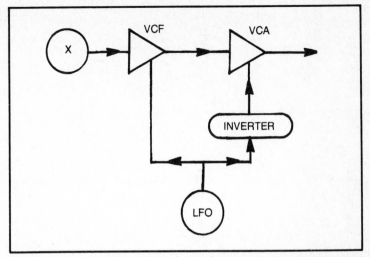

Fig. A-4. X can be any source. The inverter is optional, but makes for more unique effects. The LFO (low-frequency oscillator) should be kept below the audible range, but experimentation is warranted. A sine wave provides the smoothest results, particularly at very low frequencies. For an interesting variation, use a VCO for the control oscillator and control it with the keyboard or a sequencer, or perhaps even a second oscillator.

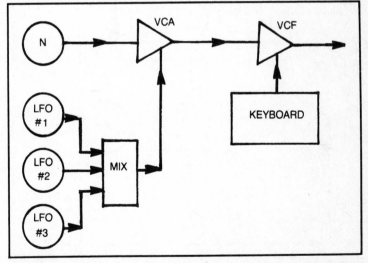

Fig. A-5. All three LFOs are tuned to different frequencies well below the audible point. LFO No. 1 could be a sawtooth, and the other two might be square or pulse waves. Experiment with various level settings on the mixer. VCOs could be used for the LFOs and controlled by the sequencer, or perhaps a function generator triggered by the keyboard. N is the noise source, and the VCF should be a band-pass filter with a narrow bandwidth.

233

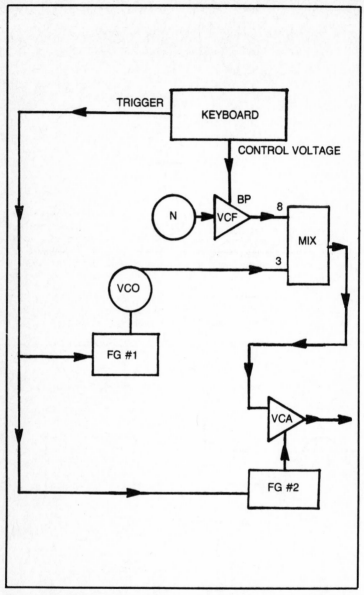

Fig. A-6. The output of this patch is a sort of pitched percussive effect. The best results are usually obtained if the output of the VCO is a sine or triangle wave, but interesting effects can also be achieved with other wave shapes. FG No. 1 should be set to a fairly quick attack with moderately long decay and no sustain. FG No. 2 should be set with practically the minimum attack time and a moderately long decay and no sustain. N is the noise source, and the voltage-controlled filter should be a band-pass type.

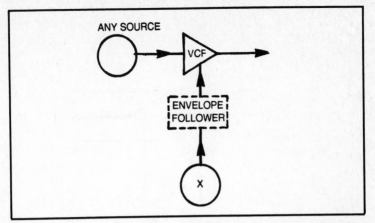

Fig. A-7. X is an external source, such as a guitar, or a sound through a microphone. The envelope follower may or may not be needed, depending on the equipment used. A VCA could be substituted for the VCF. For really unusual effects, mix the unaltered external input signal back in with the output of the synthesizer.

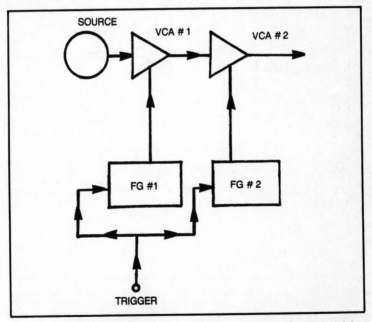

Fig. A-8. If the two function generators are set up with different attack and delay times, some very interesting and very complex patterns might occur. Remember not to let the control settings be identical (the effect would be essentially the same as using one VCA and FG), or micro mirror images of each other (the effects would tend to cancel each other). Other than that, it's free game. VCFs could be substituted for the VCAs.

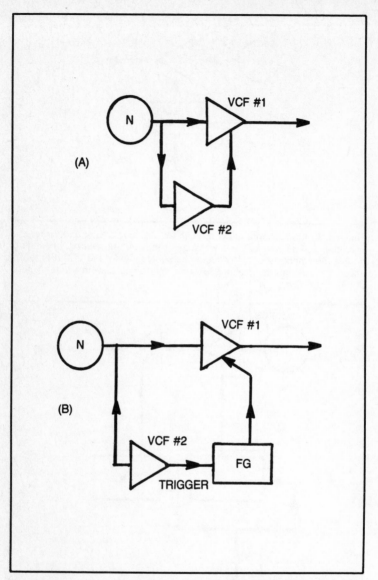

Fig. A-9. Here we have two variations on a rather simple patch. N is the noise source. In both patches, VCF No. 1 should be a band-pass filter, and VCF No. 2 should be a low-pass filter tuned to cutoff at about 6 to 10 Hz. In (A), the output of the filter will randomly fluctuate in timbre. In (B), the function generator will be randomly triggered to produce a repeating but irregularly spaced change in the timbre of the output. The version shown in (B) is more critical because if the noise source isn't filtered enough, the function generator might trigger and stay triggered. The space between trigger signals has to be longer than the time it takes for the function generator to produce its entire envelope.

Fig. A-10. This is probably the most complex patch in the book. It sounds like a robot whistling—complete with breathing sounds—but you might have other ideas. With just a little bit of twiddling, you can have an excellent steam whistle. N is the noise source. VCO No. 1 should be a whistle sound in the first place, probably a triangle or sine wave. The pitch should be somewhere near 4 to 5 kHz, and could be controlled by either the keyboard or a sequencer, or perhaps even both. VCO No. 2 should be a very low-frequency sine wave. All the points marked T are triggered n inputs and should be driven simultaneously. Function generators Nos. 1, 2 and 4 are of the attack/decay type, while Nos. 3 and 5 are ADSR generators. The settings are as follows: FG No. 1 is set at slow attack/medium fast decay. FG No. 2 is set at medium fast attack/slow decay and no sustain. FG No. 3 is set at medium attack with sharp initial decay. The sustain level is set at about the halfway point for medium slow release. FG No. 4 is set at medium slow attack with a very fast decay. FG No. 5 is set at medium fast attack with medium release. The sustain level is set about halfway for a medium slow release. VCF No. 1 is a band-pass type, and VCF No. 2 is a high-pass filter.

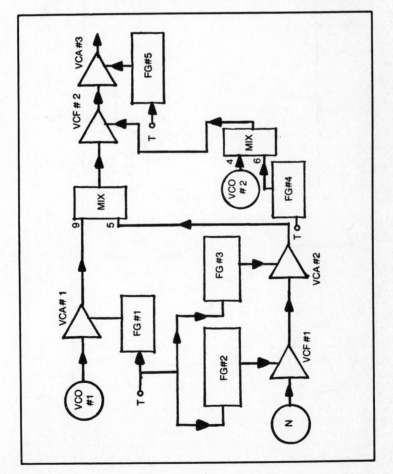

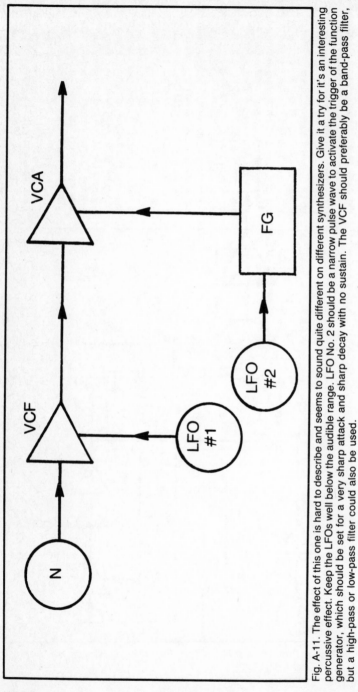

Fig. A-11. The effect of this one is hard to describe and seems to sound quite different on different synthesizers. Give it a try for it's an interesting percussive effect. Keep the LFOs well below the audible range. LFO No. 2 should be a narrow pulse wave to activate the trigger of the function generator, which should be set for a very sharp attack and sharp decay with no sustain. The VCF should preferably be a band-pass filter, but a high-pass or low-pass filter could also be used.

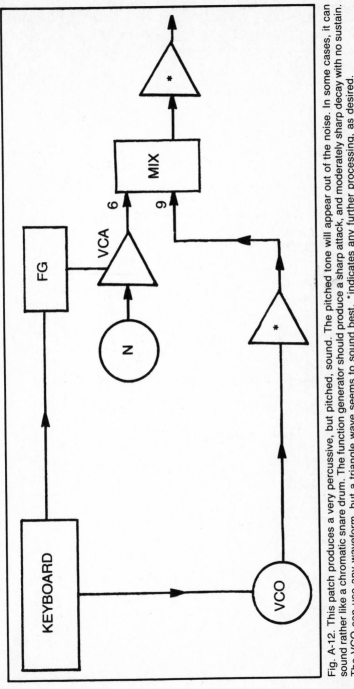

Fig. A-12. This patch produces a very percussive, but pitched, sound. The pitched tone will appear out of the noise. In some cases, it can sound rather like a chromatic snare drum. The function generator should produce a sharp attack, and moderately sharp decay with no sustain. The VCO can use any waveform, but a triangle wave seems to sound best. *indicates any further processing, as desired.

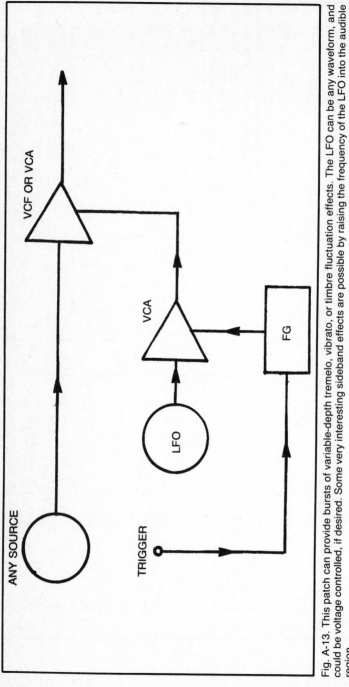

Fig. A-13. This patch can provide bursts of variable-depth tremelo, vibrato, or timbre fluctuation effects. The LFO can be any waveform, and could be voltage controlled, if desired. Some very interesting sideband effects are possible by raising the frequency of the LFO into the audible region.

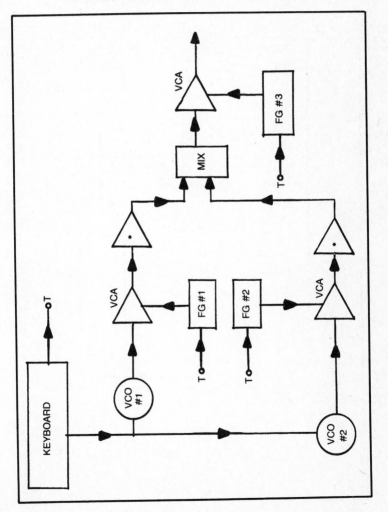

Fig. A-14. Points marked T are triggered points and should be tied together. The trigger signal from the keyboard drives all three function generators. FG No. 1 should be set with a sharp attack and slow decay. FG No. 2 should be the exact opposite—slow attack and sharp decay. The setting of FG No. 3 is more flexible, but seems to sound best with a moderate attack and decay. * indicates further processing, as desired. The end result will be a blending of two voices. Each note starts out with voice No. 1, but turns into voice No. 2. If the differences between the two voices are subtle, some very natural sounding effects can be achieved. On the other hand, some really unique sounds are possible with two contrasting voices.

241

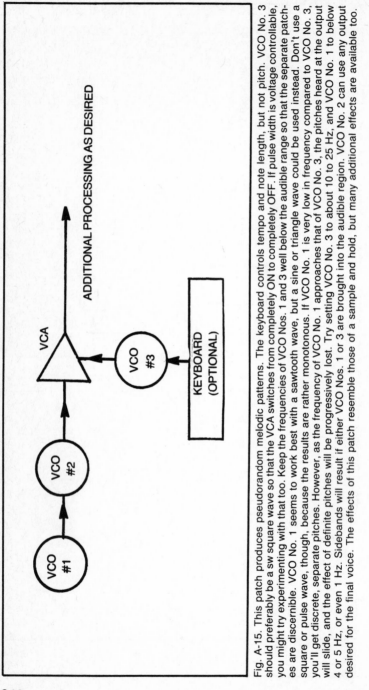

Fig. A-15. This patch produces pseudorandom melodic patterns. The keyboard controls tempo and note length, but not pitch. VCO No. 3 should preferably be a sw square wave so that the VCA switches from completely ON to completely OFF. If pulse width is voltage controllable, you might try experimenting with that too. Keep the frequencies of VCO Nos. 1 and 3 well below the audible range so that the separate patches are discernible. VCO No. 1 seems to work best with a sawtooth wave, but a sine or triangle wave could be used instead. Don't use a square or pulse wave, though, because the results are rather monotonous. If VCO No. 1 is very low in frequency compared to VCO No. 3, you'll get discrete, separate pitches. However, as the frequency of VCO No. 1 approaches that of VCO No. 3, the pitches heard at the output will slide, and the effect of definite pitches will be progressively lost. Try setting VCO No. 3 to about 10 to 25 Hz, and VCO No. 1 to below 4 or 5 Hz, or even 1 Hz. Sidebands will result if either VCO Nos. 1 or 3 are brought into the audible region. VCO No. 2 can use any output desired for the final voice. The effects of this patch resemble those of a sample and hold, but many additional effects are available too.

242

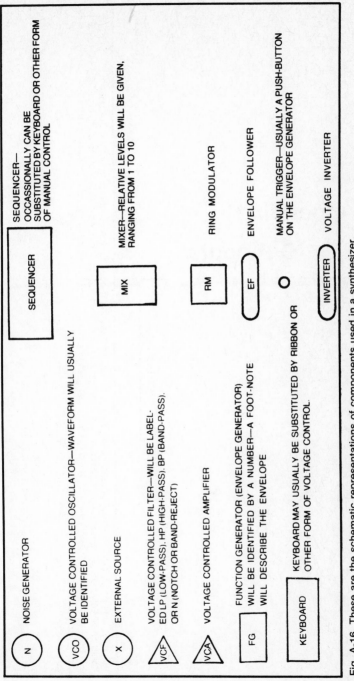

N — NOISE GENERATOR

VCO — VOLTAGE CONTROLLED OSCILLATOR—WAVEFORM WILL USUALLY BE IDENTIFIED

X — EXTERNAL SOURCE

VCF — VOLTAGE CONTROLLED FILTER—WILL BE LABEL-ED LP (LOW-PASS), HP (HIGH-PASS). BP (BAND-PASS). OR N (NOTCH OR BAND-REJECT)

VCA — VOLTAGE CONTROLLED AMPLIFIER

FG — FUNCTION GENERATOR (ENVELOPE GENERATOR) WILL BE IDENTIFIED BY A NUMBER—A FOOT-NOTE WILL DESCRIBE THE ENVELOPE

KEYBOARD — KEYBOARD MAY USUALLY BE SUBSTITUTED BY RIBBON OR OTHER FORM OF VOLTAGE CONTROL.

SEQUENCER — OCCASSIONALLY CAN BE SUBSTITUTED BY KEYBOARD OR OTHER FORM OF MANUAL CONTROL

MIX — MIXER—RELATIVE LEVELS WILL BE GIVEN, RANGING FROM 1 TO 10

RM — RING MODULATOR

EF — ENVELOPE FOLLOWER

O — MANUAL TRIGGER—USUALLY A PUSH-BUTTON ON THE ENVELOPE GENERATOR

INVERTER — VOLTAGE INVERTER

Fig. A-16. These are the schematic representations of components used in a synthesizer.

243

Appendix B
TTL IC Pinouts

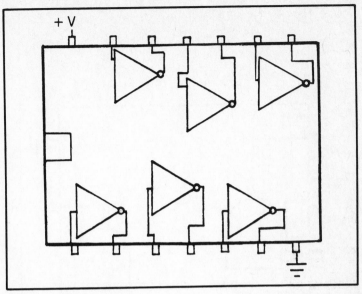

Fig. B-1. 7404 hex inverter.

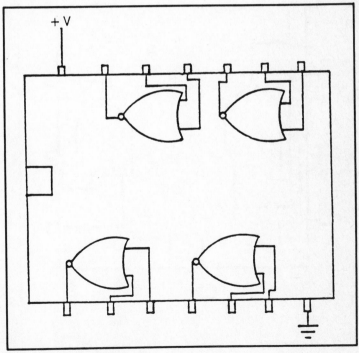

Fig. B-2. 7402 quad NOR gate.

245

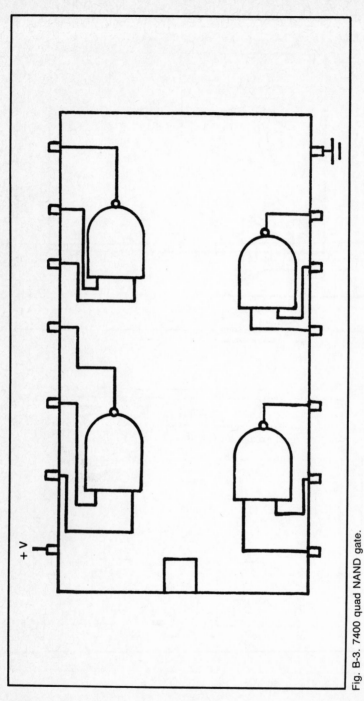

Fig. B-3. 7400 quad NAND gate.

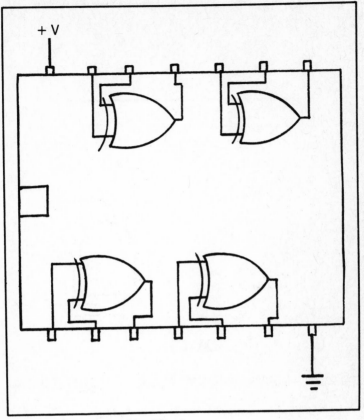

Fig. B-4. 7486 quad exclusive OR gate.

Appendix C
CMOS IC Pinouts

TTL ICs were used for the projects, simply because I had plenty available when I designed the circuits. At the time, they were the cheapest, and most readily available choice.

Today the situation has changed. CMOS ICs are becoming more and more popular for digital circuits. They are now cost competitive with TTL chips, and are often more readily available.

The biggest difference between these two logic families is in their power supply requirements. TTL gates require a tightly regulated 5 volt power source. CMOS devices, on the other hand, can operate on anything from about 3 to 15 volts. Regulation is still a good idea, but the power source is much more flexible.

For hobbyists who prefer CMOS to TTL, the next few pages will give the pin-out diagrams for suitable CMOS ICs that can be used in place of the TTL devices specified in the projects.

If you decide to use CMOS chips, be careful about static discharge, because these units can be easily damaged by a burst of static electricity.

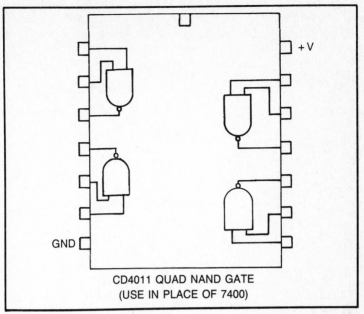

Fig. C-1. CD 4011 quad NAND gate.

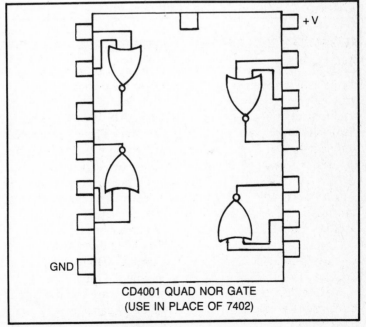

Fig. C-2. CD 4001 quad NOR gate.

249

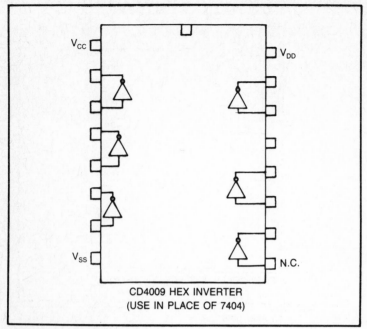

CD4009 HEX INVERTER
(USE IN PLACE OF 7404)

Fig. C-3. CD 4009 hex inverter.

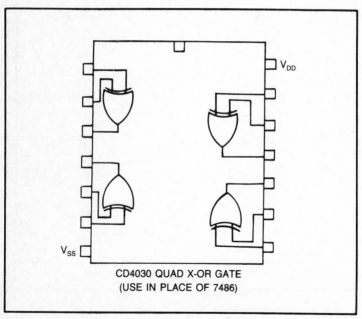

CD4030 QUAD X-OR GATE
(USE IN PLACE OF 7486)

Fig. C-4. CD 4030 quad exclusive OR gate (use in place of 7486).

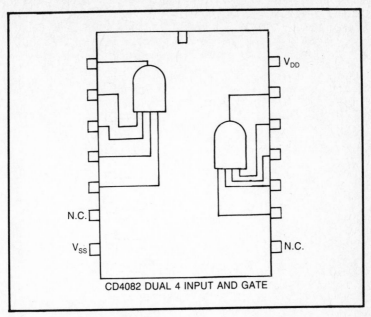

Fig. C-5. Dual 4 input AND gate.

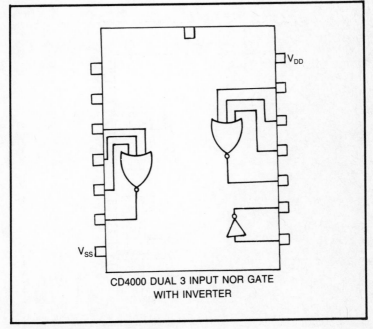

Fig. C-6. Dual 3 input NOR gate.

Index

Index

258

Other Bestsellers From TAB